MODERN CHINESE

现代中文 SECOND EDITION

WORKBOOK 1A
SIMPLIFIED CHARACTERS

BetterChinese

BetterChinese

MODERN CHINESE 现代中文
Workbook Volume 1A

Second Edition

Project Director:	James P. Lin
Editorial Consultant:	Li-Hsiang Yu Shen
Project Manager:	Angel Yeh
Assistant Editors:	Sue-Ann Ma, Christopher Peacock, and Cheuk-Yue Fung
Curriculum Advisors:	Norman Masuda and Rebecca Starr
Executive Publisher:	Chi-Kuo Shen
Illustrations:	Better World Ltd

ISBN: 978-1-60603-572-6

2 3 4 XLA 16 15 14

For more information about our products, contact us at:

United States
640 Waverley Street
Palo Alto, CA 94301
Tel: 888-384-0902
Fax: 888-384-0901
Email: usa@betterchinese.com

Contents 目录

Foreword

About the Workbook

The *Modern Chinese* workbook is designed to create opportunities for students to practice individual language skills in targeted settings as well as in holistic and applied ways. This Second Edition incorporates many suggestions based on classroom experiences. For each section in the workbook, there are numerous real-life practices focused on getting students to understand, to speak, and to write Chinese. These exercises are not only useful for achieving the objectives of each lesson, they are also designed to build on top of previous lessons. In this way students are able to establish a strong foundation in the language.

Please visit our website, http://college.betterchinese.com, to access additional resources, such as audio files for listening comprehension practices, audio recording tools, further cultural information, and additional character writing materials. The workbook is comprised of the following sections:

Vocabulary Review

Various exercises aim to help students absorb the new vocabulary introduced in each lesson. Exercises focus on character recognition and pinyin accuracy.

Character Writing Practice

Characters highlighted in the Practice section of the textbook are revisited with ample space for writing practice. Complete stroke-order sequence diagrams and radical information are also included. For further character writing practice, please visit the website to download additional character writing sheets.

Listening Comprehension

This section offers an extra opportunity to gain exposure to Chinese sentences and conversations outside of the classroom. Students answer a variety of comprehension questions after listening to short dialogues and/or narratives in Standard Mandarin. Visit our website to download the audio files for the exercises.

Speaking Practice

To encourage active production of Chinese sentences, this section prompts students to make audio recordings that role-play everyday situations they may encounter. Students can also visit our website to use our online tools to record their compositions and send them to their teacher for review. Alternatively, teachers may want to use this section in the classroom for additional speaking practice.

Structure Review

Each section provides the Structure Note formula introduced in the lesson and also exercises focusing on mastery of the grammar.

Reading Comprehension

Lesson vocabulary and Structure Notes are reviewed in passages, narratives, and other authentic materials. Questions are provided to assess students' comprehension of the material.

Writing Practice

This section provides another opportunity for students to practice writing Chinese using authentic materials. Students must draw from previously learned vocabulary and Structure Notes to compose short essays based on prompts relevant to the theme of the lesson.

祝你学习进步!
Happy Chinese learning!

UNIT 1 — LESSON 1　你好!

VOCABULARY REVIEW 1.1

I. Mark the correct tones over the pinyin for the vocabulary below. *Read the characters aloud as you mark the tones.*

1.	陈	Chen	9.	你好!	Ni hao!
2.	很	hen	10.	什么	shenme
3.	叫	jiao	11.	他	ta
4.	老师	laoshi	12.	同学们	tongxuemen
5.	孙	Sun	13.	我	wo
6.	吗	ma	14.	谢谢	xiexie
7.	名字	mingzi	15.	也	ye
8.	呢	ne	16.	再见	zaijian

II. Match the Chinese vocabulary below with the corresponding English meanings.

1. 谢谢　　　•　　　　•　a. classmates

2. 名字　　　•　　　　•　b. goodbye

3. 什么　　　•　　　　•　c. teacher

4. 再见　　　•　　　　•　d. thank you

5. 老师　　　•　　　　•　e. Miss Chen

6. 陈小姐　　•　　　　•　f. name

7. 同学们　　•　　　　•　g. what

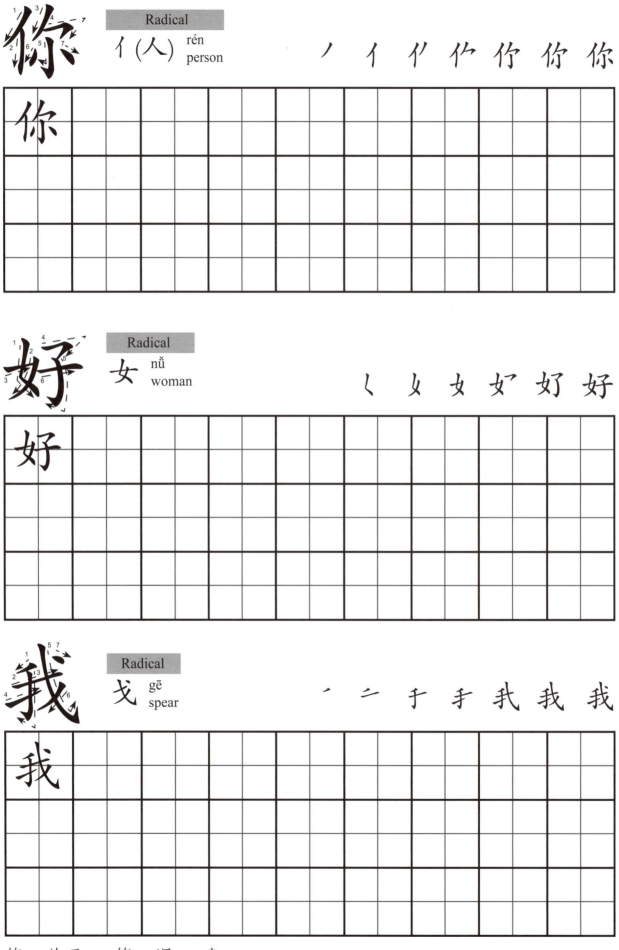

Radical

亻(人) rén person

ノ 亻 亻 亻 你 你 你

Radical

女 nǚ woman

く 乆 女 女 妤 好

Radical

戈 gē spear

一 二 于 于 我 我 我

很

Radical

彳 chì step

丿 ㇒㇒ 彳 彳𠃌 彳ヨ 彳彐 很 很 很

很

也

Radical

乙 yǐ second heavenly stem

𠃌 𠃌丨 也

也

老

Radical

老 lǎo old

一 十 土 耂 耂 老

老

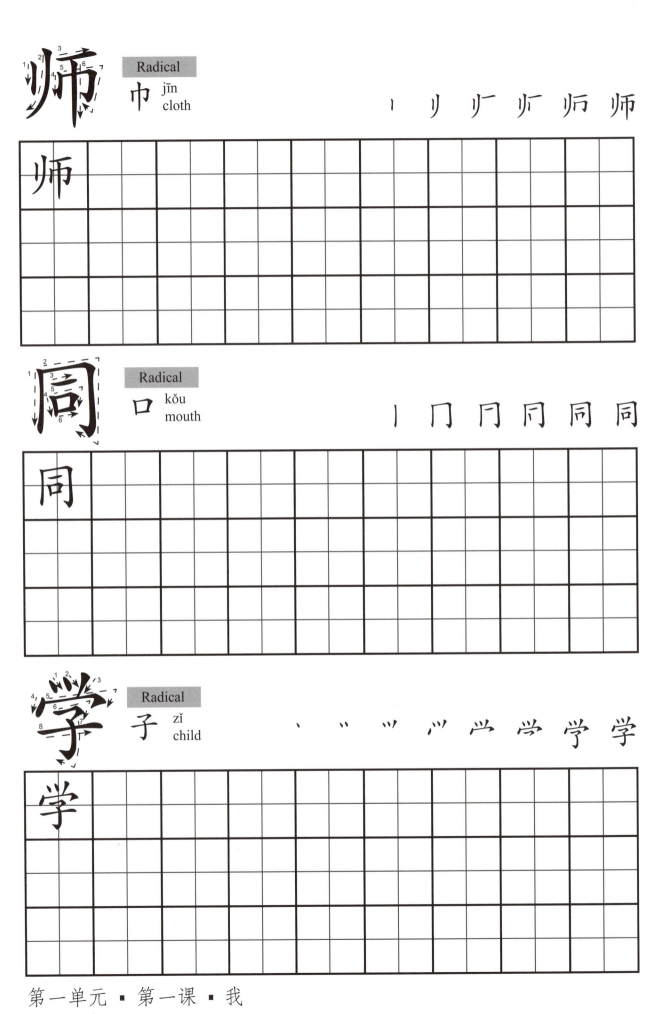

师　Radical　巾　jīn　cloth　　丿丿丿丆丆师师

同　Radical　口　kǒu　mouth　　丨冂冂同同同

学　Radical　子　zǐ　child　　丶丷丷丷丷兴学学学

们

Radical

亻(人) rén
person

ノ 亻 亻 个 们

们									

叫

Radical

口 kǒu
mouth

丨 口 口 叫 叫

叫									

名

Radical

口 kǒu
mouth

ノ 夕 夕 夕 名 名

名									

字

Radical
子 zǐ
child

、 ﾉ 宀 宀 宁 字

字

他

Radical
亻(人) rén
person

ノ 亻 亻 仲 他

他

见

Radical
见 jiàn
see

丨 冂 贝 见

见

LISTENING COMPREHENSION 1.1

I. Choose the sentence that matches what you hear.

1. A. Nǐ hǎo. Wǒ jiào Sūn Mǎlì. Nǐ jiào shénme míngzi?
   B. Nǐ hǎo. Wǒ jiào Sūn Mǎlì. Nǐ xìng shénme?
   C. Nǐ hǎo. Wǒ jiào Chén Dàdōng. Nǐ jiào shénme míngzi?
   D. Nǐ hǎo. Wǒ jiào Chén Dàdōng. Nǐ xìng shénme?

2. A. Lǎoshī, nín hǎo ma?
   B. Dàdōng, nínhǎo ma?
   C. Chén xiānsheng, nín hǎo ma?
   D. Sūn tàitai, nín hǎo ma?

   老师 您好吗

3. A. Nǐ jiào Sūn Mǎlì ma?
   B. Wǒ jiào Sūn Mǎlì ma?
   C. Tā jiào Sūn Mǎlì ma?
   D. Tāmen jiào Sūn Mǎlì ma?

4. A. Xièxie, nǐ ne?
   B. Xièxie, wǒ hěn hǎo.
   C. Wǒ hěn hǎo, nǐ ne?
   D. Wǒ hěn hǎo, xièxie.

5. A. Chén xiānsheng, nǐ hǎo!
   B. Sūn xiānsheng, nǐ hǎo!
   C. Chén xiānsheng, zàijiàn!
   D. Sūn xiānsheng, zàijiàn!

II. Choose the best response to the sentence(s) you hear.

1. A. Xièxie.
   B. Nǐ ne?
   C. Wǒ jiào Chén Dàdōng.
   D. Wǒ hěn hǎo.

2. A. Nǐ hǎo ma?
   B. Lǎoshī hěn hǎo.
   C. Sūn Mǎlì, zàijiàn.
   D. Tā jiào Chén Dàdōng.

3. A. Wǒ jiào Dàdōng.
   B. Xièxie, lǎoshī.
   C. Wǒ hěn hǎo.
   D. Wǒ yě hěn hǎo.

4. A. Zàijiàn, lǎoshī!
   B. Nǐ jiào Dàdōng.
   C. Nǐ ne?
   D. Lǎoshī jiào Liú Dàdōng.

5. A. Xièxie.
   B. Wǒ jiào Liú Dàdōng. Tā jiào Chén Dàdōng.
   C. Sūn Mǎlì, zàijiàn.
   D. Sūn Mǎlì, nǐ hǎo ma?

III. Choose the best answer for each question, based on each dialogue.

1. Which of the following statements is true?

    A. The man's name is Chen Mali.

    B. Chen Dadong is talking to his teacher.

    C. The man is the woman's teacher.

    D. The woman bids farewell to the man.

2. Which of the following statements is true?

    A. The man asks for the woman's name.

    B. The woman asks for the man's name.

    C. The woman's surname is Sun.

    D. The woman is not very well.

3. Which of the following statements is true?

    A. The man is a teacher.

    B. The woman is a teacher.

    C. The woman's surname is Liu.

    D. They are saying hello to each other.

4. Which of the following statements is true?

    A. The man asks if the woman is well.

    B. They are talking about a teacher.

    C. The woman's surname is Liu.

    D. The man's surname is Liu.

5. Which of the following statements is true?

    A. The man is saying goodbye to the woman.

    B. The woman is saying goodbye to the man.

    C. The man's surname is Chen.

    D. The woman's surname is Chen.

I. Listen to the audio recording. Say aloud an appropriate response to each sentence you hear. Use the space below to make note of your ideas, if necessary.

1. Your response: _____

2. Your response: _____

3. Your response: _____

4. Your response: _____

5. Your response: _____

II. Listen to the audio recording. For each response, identify and say the appropriate preceding sentence. Use the space below to make note of your ideas, if necessary.

1. Your preceding sentence: 你好吗？　　　　我很好。謝
   我很好。

2. Your preceding sentence: 同学们,再见　　　老师 再见

3. Your preceding sentence: 你好　　　Chén dàdōng 你好

4. Your preceding sentence: 你好叫什么名字　我叫 sūn mǎlǐ

5. Your preceding sentence: 她 ne　　　她也很好
   我很好

STRUCTURE REVIEW 1.1

I. Complete the following Structure Note practices.

Structure Note 1.1: Use an adjective phrase to describe a subject.

> Subject + Adjective Phrase

A. Write the following sentences in Chinese. Record your answers in both pinyin and characters.

	Pinyin	Characters
1. She is well.		
2. The teacher is well.		
3. The classmates are well.		
4. Mr. Chen is well.		
5. Miss Sun is well.		

Structure Note 1.2. Use 们 to convert a pronoun or noun (people only) to its plural form.

> Pronoun / Noun (people) + 们

B. Write the following sentences in Chinese. Record your answers in both pinyin and characters.

	Pinyin	Characters
1. We		
2. You (plural)		
3. They (male)		
4. They (female)		
5. The teachers		

Structure Note 1.3: Use 也 to express "also."

> Subject + 也 + Verb / Adjective Phrase

C. Write the following sentences in Chinese. Record your answers in both pinyin and characters.

	Pinyin	Characters
1. She is also well.	tā yě hěn hǎo	她也很好
2. The teacher is also well.	lǎo shī yě hěn hǎo	老
3. The students are also well.	tóng xué mén yě hěn hǎo	
4. Miss Chen is also well.	chén xiān sheng yě hěn hǎo	
5. Ms. Sun is also well.	sūn xiān sheng yě hěn hǎo	

Structure Note 1.4: Use 吗 to turn a statement into a question.

> Statement + 吗 ?

D. Write the following sentences in Chinese. Record your answers in both pinyin and characters.

	Pinyin	Characters
1. Is she well?		
2. Are you (polite) well?		
3. Is the teacher well?		
4. Are the students well?		
5. Is Chen Dadong well?		

Structure Note 1.5: Use 呢 to ask "What about...?"

> Statement + Noun/Pronoun + 呢 ?

E. Write the following sentences in Chinese. Record your answers in both pinyin and characters.

	Pinyin	Characters
1. What about me?		
2. What about them?		
3. What about the teacher?		
4. What about the students?		
5. What about Mrs. Sun?		

Structure Note 1.6: Use 叫 to state one's name.

> Subject + 叫 + Name

F. Write the following sentences in Chinese. Record your answers in both pinyin and characters.

	Pinyin	Characters
1. Her name is Sun Mali.	_____	_____
2. His name is Chen Dadong.	_____	_____
3. My name is Chen Dadong.	_____	_____
4. Her name is Chen Li.	_____	_____
5. The teacher's name is Sun Mali.	_____	_____

Structure Note 1.7: Use 什么 to ask "what?" questions.

> Subject + Verb + 什么 + Noun ?

G. Write the following sentences in Chinese. Record your answers in both pinyin and characters.

	Pinyin	Characters
1. What is my name?	_____	_____
2. What is her name?	_____	_____
3. What is your (polite) name?	_____	_____
4. What are their names?	_____	_____
5. What is the teacher's name?	_____	_____

II. Complete the dialogues using the words suggested in the parentheses provided.
Read your answers aloud.

1. A: _____? (吗)

   B: 我很好，谢谢。

2. A: 老师好吗？

   B: _____。(很)

3. A: 我叫孙玛丽。_____? (呢)

   B: 我叫陈大东。

4. A: 他叫陈大东。

   B: _____。(也)

5. A: 你们好吗？

   B: _____。(们)

6. A: _____? (叫什么)

   B: 我叫陈大东。

7. A: 老师叫什么名字？

   B: _____。(叫)

I. Choose the best answers to fill in the blanks.

1. 你 ＿＿＿ 好！我 ＿＿＿ 陈大东。

 A. 很……再
 B. 们……叫
 C. 见……陈
 D. 她……谢谢

2. ＿＿＿ 很好。我 ＿＿＿ 很好。

 A. 老师……也
 B. 我……吗
 C. 她……谢谢
 D. 好……呢

3. ＿＿＿ 叫陈大东。你 ＿＿＿？

 A. 你……呢
 B. 我……也很好
 C. 我……叫什么名字
 D. 她……王

4. ＿＿＿ 先生，你好 ＿＿＿？

 A. 再见……很好
 B. 他……呢
 C. 他……孙
 D. 陈……吗

5. ＿＿＿ 叫孙玛丽。你 ＿＿＿？

 A. 他们……呢
 B. 你……也
 C. 我……呢
 D. 老师……很好

II. Read the dialogues and answer the following True or False questions.

A.

Person A: 老师好！
Person B: 你好！
Person A: 我叫孙玛丽。您叫什么名字？
Person B: 我叫刘大东。

1. T F Person B is a teacher.

2. T F Person A is called Mali.

3. T F Person A thanks Person B.

4. T F Person A's surname is Sun.

5. T F Person B's surname is Liu.

B.

Person A: 你好吗？
Person B: 我很好，谢谢。你呢？
Person A: 我也很好。
Person B: 老师也好吗？
Person A: 她也很好。

1. T F Person A asks if Person B is well.

2. T F Person A thanks Person B.

3. T F Person B is well.

4. T F Person B does not ask if Person A is well.

5. T F The teacher they are talking about is female.

III. Identify and circle the surnames on these namecards. Write the pinyin of each surname in the space provided.

陈 彬
经理

电话: 63330040 63332970
传真: 63332970
手机: 13051272126
电邮: cbb_by@hotmail.com
邮编: 100054
北京市台区某户堂东街

京五旅行社有限责任公司

1. Pinyin: _____

中国工商银行 北京市昌平支行
沙河分理处

刘兵 主任

地址: 昌平区沙河巩华镇■号
电话: 69731■   手机: 136013666■

2. Pinyin: _____

河北孙大灯工贸有限公司

孙大灯

地址：河北虎口汽车农机配件城中区8栋5号
电话: 0312-6853022   传真：6856565
手机：   E-mail：qiye@zggp.com.cn
网址：http://hbsunda.zggp.com.cn

3. Pinyin: _____

广安市青年旅行社

陈建波

地址：四川广安市保真场三楼
电话：86-826-2345315   2292889
手机：13603326709 13982638588
传真：86-826-2338443
http://: www.ga-ly.com
E-mail: webmaster@ga-ly.com
QQ语音: 81686105

主要景点：邓小平故里   华蓥山风景区   巴人文化   思源广场

4. Pinyin: _____

孙 健 杭州部经理
15607617719

L-HAN-GJ00010

海南航空国际旅行社
HAINAN AIR INTERNATIONAL TRAVEL SERVICE

地址:海口市和平大道19号   邮编P.C.：570208
Add:No.19,HePing Rd,Haikou City,Hainan,China
电话Tel:0898-66268769   66194363
传真Fax:0898-66194393   Q Q：459972170
E-mail:sunjianfhm@yahoo.com.cn

5. Pinyin: _____

I. Write a letter to a penpal, using paragraphs and the basic letter format below. This letter will be incomplete for now, but you will expand upon it as you learn more Chinese. Be prepared to read your letter aloud in class.

你好 :
(Greeting)

我 叫 村田美菜 。
(Introduce your name)

你 叫什么名字 ?
(Ask what your penpal's name is)

村田美菜
(Sign your name)

UNIT 1 — LESSON 2

VOCABULARY REVIEW 1.2

I. Mark the correct tones over the pinyin for the vocabulary below. *Read the characters aloud as you mark the tones.*

1. 不 bú
2. 大 da
3. 多 duō
4. 二 èr
5. 国 guó
6. 加拿大 Jiānádà
7. 九 jiǔ

8. 美国 Meiguó
9. 美国人 Meiguó ren
10. 哪 nǎ
11. 人 ren
12. 十 shí
13. 是 shì
14. 岁 suì

II. Complete the calendar by filling in characters for each date. *Read the numbers aloud as you fill in the blanks.*

December 2010						
SUN	MON	TUE	WED	THU	FRI	SAT
			一	二	三	四
五	六	七	八	九	十	十一
十二	十三	十四	十五	十六	十七	十八
十九	二十	二十一	二十二	二十三	二十四	二十五 Christmas Day
二十六	二十七	二十八	二十九	三十	三十一 New Year's Eve	

III. Write the pinyin of the name of each country next to its flag. Refer to the Optional Vocabulary for additional country names. *Read your answers aloud.*

1. 美国 měi guó

2. 中国 zhōng guó

3. 加拿大 jiā ná dà

4. 日本 rì běn

5. 英国 yīng guó

IV. Write the pinyin for the names of the Zodiac animals in the picture below. Refer to the Language Notes section in the Textbook for the names of the animals. *Read your answers aloud.*

1. _____

2. _____

3. _____

4. _____

5. _____

6. _____

7. _____

8. _____

9. _____

10. _____

11. _____

12. _____

多

Radical

夕 xī
evening

丿 夕 夕 夕 多 多

多									

大

Radical

大 dà
big

一 ナ 大

大									

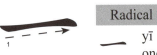

Radical

一 yī
one

一

一									

二

Radical

二 èr
two

一 二

二

三

Radical

一 yī
one

一 二 三

三

四

Radical

口 wéi
enclosure

丨 冂 冂 四 四

四

Radical

二 èr
two

一 丁 五 五

五									

Radical

八 bā
eight

、 亠 六 六

六									

Radical

一 yī
one

一 七

七									

Radical

八 bā
eight

ノ 八

八

Radical

ノ piě
slash

ノ 九

九

Radical

十 shí
ten

一 十

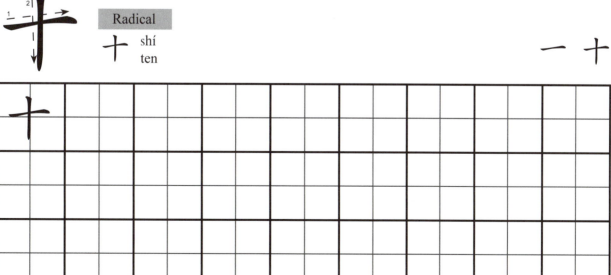

岁

山 shān
mountain

丶 山 山 屵 岁 岁

岁									

是

Radical

日 rì
sun

丶 冂 曰 日 旦 早 旱 昰 是

是									

人

Radical

人 rén
person

丿 人

人									

LISTENING COMPREHENSION 1.2

I. Listen to the audio recording and answer the following questions in English or pinyin. (Refer to the Optional Vocabulary section for additional country names).

1. A. How old is she? _____

    B. What country is she from?_____

2. A. What is his name? _____

    B. How old is he? _____

    C. What country is he from? _____

3. A. What is her name? _____

    B. How old is she? _____

    C. What country is she from?_____

4. A. How old is he? _____

    B. What country is he from? _____

5. A. What is her name? _____

    B. How old is she? _____

    C. What country is she from?_____

II. Choose the best response to the sentence(s) you hear. (Refer to the Optional Vocabulary section for additional country names).

1. A. Wǒ bú shì Yīngguó rén.

   B. Shì, wǒ bú shì Fǎguó rén.

   C. Bú shì, wǒ bú shì Fǎguó rén.

   D. Nǐ shì bu shì Fǎguó rén?

2. A. Tā jiào Sūn Mǎlì.

   B. Tā liù suì.

   C. Tā duō dà?

   D. Tā sān shí bā suì.

3. A. Tā shì Yīngguó rén ma?

   B. Tā shì bu shì Fǎguó rén?

   C. Tā bú shì Zhōngguó rén.

   D. Tā shì Zhōngguó rén.

4. A. Tā duō dà?

   B. Tā bā shí wǔ suì.

   C. Tā qī suì.

   D. Tā jiǔ suì ma?

5. A. Wǒ yě bú shì Měiguó rén.

   B. Nǐ shì Měiguó rén?

   C. Wǒ shì Zhōngguó rén.

   D. Wǒ shì nǎ guó rén?

III. Choose the best answer for each question, based on each dialogue. (Refer to the Optional Vocabulary section for additional country names).

1. Which of the following statements is true?

    A. The man is 27 years old.

    B. The woman is 27 years old.

    C. The man is 29 years old.

    D. The woman is 29 years old.

2. Which of the following statements is true?

    A. The teacher is 58 years old.

    B. The teacher is 56 years old.

    C. The teacher is 60 years old.

    D. The teacher is 85 years old.

3. Which of the following statements is true?

    A. The woman is American.

    B. The man is American.

    C. The woman is French.

    D. The man is French.

4. Which of the following statements is true?

    A. Chen Dadong is French.

    B. The woman is French.

    C. The man is Chen Dadong.

    D. The woman asks if the man is French.

5. Which of the following statements is true?

    A. Both speakers are Chinese.

    B. Only the man is Chinese.

    C. Only the woman is Chinese.

    D. The woman is not Chinese.

I. Listen to the audio recording. Say aloud an appropriate response to each sentence that you hear. (Refer to the Optional Vocabulary section for additional country names). Use the space below to make note of your ideas, if necessary.

1. Your response: _____

2. Your response: _____

3. Your response: _____

4. Your response: _____

5. Your response: _____

II. Listen to the audio recording. For each response that you hear, identify and say aloud the appropriate preceding sentence. (Refer to the Optional Vocabulary section for additional country names). Use the space below to make note of your ideas, if necessary.

1. Your preceding sentence: _____

2. Your preceding sentence: _____

3. Your preceding sentence: _____

4. Your preceding sentence: _____

5. Your preceding sentence: _____

STRUCTURE REVIEW 1.2

I. Complete the following Structure Note practices.

Structure Note 1.8: Use 多大 to ask about someone's age.

> Subject + 多大 ?

A. Write the following sentences in Chinese. Record your answers in both pinyin and characters.

	Pinyin	Characters
1. How old are you (polite)?		
2. How old are you (plural)?		
3. How old is the teacher?		
4. How old is Miss Sun?		
5. How old is Mr Chen?		

Structure Note 1.9: Add 岁 after a number to state one's age.

> Subject + Number + 岁

B. Write the following sentences in Chinese. Record your answers in both pinyin and characters.

	Pinyin	Characters
1. He is 5 years old.		
2. She is 14 years old.		
3. The students are 10 years old.		
4. Mrs. Chen is 60 years old.		
5. Mr. Sun is 71 years old.		

Structure Note 1.10: Use 是 to indicate equivalency.

> Subject + 是 + Predicate

C. Write the following sentences in Chinese. Record your answers in both pinyin and characters. (Refer to the Optional Vocabulary if necessary).

	Pinyin	Characters
1. She is Chinese.	_____	_____
2. They are British.	_____	_____
3. The teacher is French.	_____	_____
4. Mr. Liu is American.	_____	_____
5. Miss Sun is Canadian.	_____	_____

Structure Note 1.11: Use 哪国人 to ask about nationality and country + 人 to state nationality.

> Subject + 是 + 哪国人 ?

D. Write the following sentences in Chinese. Record your answers in both pinyin and characters.

	Pinyin	Characters
1. Which country are you (polite) from?	_____	_____
2. Which country are you (plural) from?	_____	_____
3. Which country are they from?	_____	_____
4. Which country is Teacher Liu from?	_____	_____
5. Which country is Miss Chen from?	_____	_____

Structure Note 1.12: Use 不 to negate a verb.

> Subject + 不 + Verb Phrase

E. Write the following sentences in Chinese. Record your answers in both pinyin and characters. (Refer to the Optional Vocabulary if necessary).

	Pinyin	Characters
1. I'm not a teacher.	_____	_____
2. He is not Chinese.	_____	_____
3. The teacher is not Canadian.	_____	_____
4. Miss Liu is not French.	_____	_____
5. Ms. Sun is not American.	_____	_____

Structure Note 1.13: Use Verb + 不 + Verb to form affirmative-negative questions.

> Subject + Verb + 不 + Verb + Noun Phrase

F. Write the following sentences in Chinese. Record your answers in both pinyin and characters. (Refer to the Optional Vocabulary if necessary).

	Pinyin	Characters
1. Is he a teacher?		
2. Are you Chinese?		
3. Is the teacher Canadian?		
4. Is Mr. Liu French?		
5. Is Mrs. Sun American?		

Structure Note 1.14: Use Verb or 不 + Verb to answer affirmative-negative questions.

> (Verb +) affirmative statement / 不 (+ Verb) + negative statement

G. Write the following sentences in Chinese. Record your answers in both pinyin and characters. (Refer to the Optional Vocabulary if necessary).

	Pinyin	Characters
1. No, he is not American.		
2. Yes, they are Chinese.		
3. No, I am not 40 years old.		
4. Yes, Mr. Chen is British.		
5. Yes, we are Canadian.		

READING COMPREHENSION 1.2

I. The tables below show the gold medal rankings for participating countries at the Beijing 2008 Olympics. In each table, the first column indicates the ranking, the second column shows the names of countries or regions, and the third column indicates the number of gold medals awarded.

排名	国家/地区	金牌
1	中国	51
2	美国	36
3	俄罗斯	23
4	英国	19
5	德国	16
6	澳大利亚	14
7	韩国	13
8	日本	9
9	意大利	8
10	法国	7

排名	国家/地区	金牌
11	乌克兰	7
12	荷兰	7
13	牙买加	5
14	西班牙	5
15	肯尼亚	5
16	白俄罗斯	4
17	罗马尼亚	4
18	埃塞俄比亚	4
19	加拿大	3
20	波兰	3

1. Circle the names of countries that you can read in Chinese. Write the English names of those countries next to their Chinese names. (Refer to the Optional Vocabulary if necessary).

2. State how many gold medals each of the countries you identified won. Use the space below to make note of your ideas.

Example:
中国　　　 : 五十一
Zhōngguó : wǔ shí yī

_____   _____   _____

_____   _____   _____

_____   _____   _____

_____   _____   _____

_____   _____   _____

II. Choose the best answers to fill in the blanks. Refer to the Optional Vocabulary if necessary.

1. 我二 ＿＿ 三岁。你 ＿＿ 二十三岁吗？

    A. 呢……再
    B. 岁……也
    C. 多……很
    D. 十……也

2. 老师 ＿＿ 美国人。他 ＿＿ 中国人？

    A. 是……什么
    B. 不是……是不是
    C. 是……呢
    D. 哪国……吗

3. 他是 ＿＿。她呢？她是 ＿＿ 人？

    A. 美国人……哪国
    B. 美国……中国
    C. 国……什么
    D. 哪国……美国

4. 她 ＿＿ 孙玛丽吗？她是不是美国人 ＿＿？

    A. 叫……什么
    B. 也……哪
    C. 很……吗
    D. 叫……None

5. 老师四十 ＿＿ 岁。他 ＿＿ 中国人。

    A. 十……再
    B. 五……是
    C. 见……不
    D. 谢……叫

III. Read the dialogues and answer the following True or False questions. Refer to the Optional Vocabulary if necessary.

A.

Person A: 老师，您多大？
Person B: 我四十六岁。你呢？
Person A: 我二十二岁。您是哪国人？
Person B: 我是中国人。你也是中国人吗？
Person A: 不是。我是英国人。

1.　　T　　(F)　　Person A is a teacher

2.　　T　　(F)　　Person A is 44 years old.

3.　　T　　(F)　　Person B is 22 years old.

4.　　(T)　　F　　Person A is British.

5.　　(T)　　F　　Person B is Chinese.

B.

Person A: 我叫陈大东。你叫什么名字？
Person B: 我叫孙玛丽。大东，你是加拿大人吗？
Person A: 是，我是加拿大人。
Person B: 我十九岁。你也十九岁吗？
Person A: 不。我二十岁。

1.　　T　　F　　Person B is Mali.

2.　　T　　F　　They are both American.

3.　　T　　F　　Dadong is older than Mali.

4.　　T　　F　　Dadong is not 21 years old yet.

5.　　T　　F　　Mali is 18 years old.

WRITING PRACTICE 1.2

I. Use Chinese characters to fill in as many of the blanks as you can in the form below.

中华人民共和国签证申请表

VISA APPLICATION FORM OF THE PEOPLE'S REPUBLIC OF CHINA

1、外文姓 Surname: 外文名 Given name:	照片 Photo

2、中文名 Chinese name (If any)	3、曾用名 Former name (If any)	

4、出生日期 Date of birth _____ 年 year _____ 月 month _____ 日 day	5、出生地 Place of birth	6、性别 Sex: 男/M ☐ 女/F ☐

7、国籍 Nationality	8、曾有过何国籍 Former nationality	9、职业 Occupation

II. Continue writing your letter to your penpal using the format below. This letter will be incomplete for now, but you will expand upon it as you learn more Chinese. Be prepared to read your letter aloud in class.

_____ :
(Your penpal's name)

_____ 。
(Greet and tell him/her your age.)

_____ 。
(Ask his/her age.)

_____ 。
(Tell him/her your nationality.)

_____ 。
(Ask his/her nationality.)

_____
(Sign your name)

UNIT 2 — LESSON 1

VOCABULARY REVIEW 2.1

I. Mark the correct tones over the pinyin for the vocabulary below. *Read the characters aloud as you mark the tones.*

1.	爸爸	baba	9.	两	liang
2.	宠物	chongwu	10.	妈妈	mama
3.	哥哥	gege	11.	猫	mao
4.	狗	gou	12.	没有	meiyou
5.	和	he	13.	人	ren
6.	几	ji	14.	只 (measure word)	zhi
7.	家	jia	15.	喜欢	xihuan
8.	可是	keshi			

II. Below is a photo of Victoria Brown's family. Fill in the blanks with the pinyin for the titles of her family members.

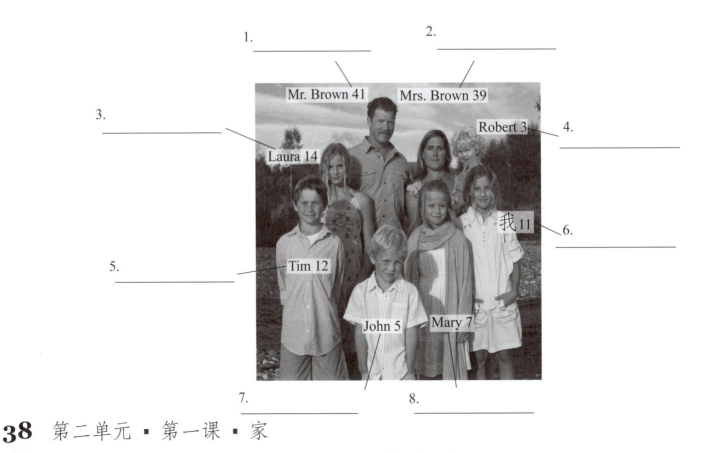

1. _____ 2. _____

3. _____

Mr. Brown 41   Mrs. Brown 39

Robert 3   4. _____

Laura 14

我 11   6. _____

5. _____   Tim 12

John 5   Mary 7

7. _____   8. _____

III. Write the pinyin for the titles of family members in the family trees below. Refer to the Language Notes section in the Textbook for the titles not covered in the Vocabulary section.

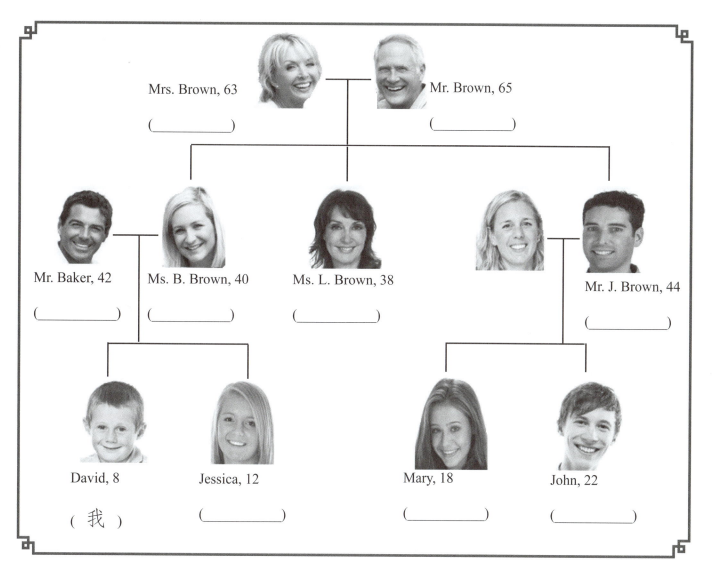

Mrs. Brown, 63
(   )

Mr. Brown, 65
(   )

Mr. Baker, 42
(   )

Ms. B. Brown, 40
(   )

Ms. L. Brown, 38
(   )

Mr. J. Brown, 44
(   )

David, 8
(我)

Jessica, 12
(   )

Mary, 18
(   )

John, 22
(   )

1. From David's perspective:

Imagine you are David.
Give an introduction of your family members. Say your introduction aloud.

For example:

Jessica 是我的姐姐。
Jessica shì wǒ de jiějie.

2. From Mary's perspective:

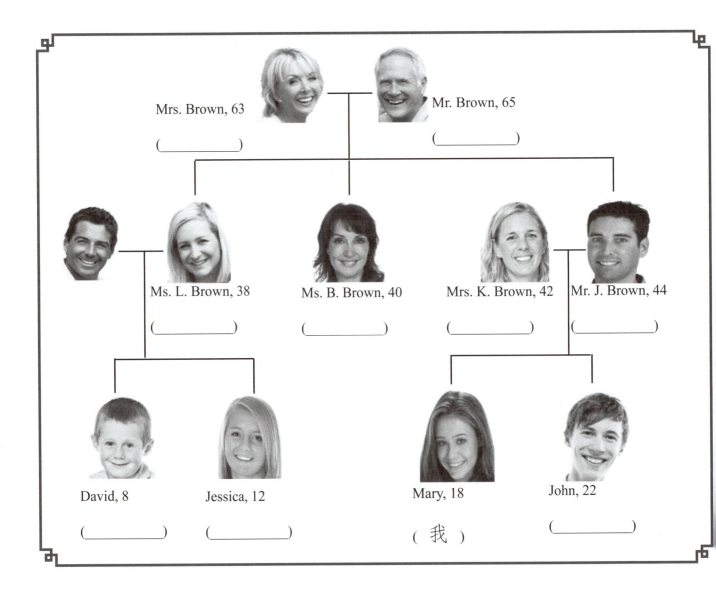

Mrs. Brown, 63 (＿＿＿＿＿)   Mr. Brown, 65 (＿＿＿＿＿＿)

Ms. L. Brown, 38 (＿＿＿＿＿)   Ms. B. Brown, 40 (＿＿＿＿＿)   Mrs. K. Brown, 42 (＿＿＿＿＿)   Mr. J. Brown, 44 (＿＿＿＿＿)

David, 8 (＿＿＿＿＿)   Jessica, 12 (＿＿＿＿＿)   Mary, 18 （我）   John, 22 (＿＿＿＿＿)

Imagine you are Mary.
Give an introduction of your family members. Say your introduction aloud.

For example:
John 是我的哥哥。
John shì wǒ de gēge.

CHARACTER WRITING PRACTICE 2.1

这

Radical
辶 chuò
walk

丶 ㇋ ㇋ 文 文 议 这

这

爸

Radical
父 fù
father

丿 八 父 父 父 爸 爸 爸

爸

妈

Radical
女 nǚ
woman

㇄ 女 女 妈 妈 妈

妈

和

Radical

口 kǒu
mouth

丿 二 千 禾 禾 禾 和 和

和

家

Radical

宀 mián
roof

丶 丶 宀 宀 宁 宁 宇 宇 家 家

家

有

Radical

月 yuè
moon

一 ナ 才 有 有 有

有

几

Radical

几 jī table

丿 几

几

个

Radical

人 rén person

丿 人 个

个

的

Radical

白 bái white

丿 亻 白 白 白 的 的 的

的

Radical

宀 mián
roof

丶 丷 宀 宁 宇 宠 宠 宠

宠											

Radical

牛 niú
cow

丿 ㇀ 牛 牛 牜 牝 物 物

物											

没

Radical

氵(水) shuǐ
water

丶 丶 氵 氵 沪 沿 没

没											

可

Radical
口 kǒu
mouth

一 丁 丌 口 可

可									

两

Radical
一 yī
one

一 厂 冂 丙 丙 两 两

两									

只

Radical
口 kǒu
mouth

丶 口 口 尸 只

只									

I. Choose the picture that best illustrates what you hear.

1. A. 　　B. 　　C.

2. A. 　　B. 　　C.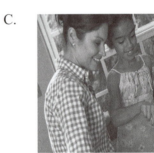

3. A. 　　B. 　　C.

4. A. 　　B. 　　C.

5. A. 　　B. 　　C.

II. Choose the best response to the sentence(s) you hear.

1. A. Tā jiā yǒu wǔ ge rén.

   B. Wǒ jiā yǒu wǔ ge rén.

   C. Tā jiā méiyǒu chǒngwù.

   D. Wǒ jiā méiyǒu chǒngwù.

2. A. Méiyǒu.

   B. Bú shì.

   C. Yǒu sān ge rén.

   D. Yǒu méiyǒu.

3. A. Tā jiā yǒu sì ge rén.

   B. Tā jiā yǒu chǒngwù.

   C. Tā jiā yǒu liǎng zhī gǒu.

   D. Tā jiā méiyǒu rén.

4. A. Méiyǒu gǒu, yǒu māo.

   B. Yǒu liǎng zhī māo.

   C. Méiyǒu māo.

   D. Yǒu sì ge rén.

5. A. Méiyǒu.

   B. Bú shì.

   C. Yǒu sān ge rén.

   D. Yǒu chǒngwù ma?

III. Choose the best answer for each question, based on each dialogue.

1. Which of the following statements is true?

   A. There are 3 people in the man's family.

   B. There are 4 people in the man's family.

   C. There are 4 people in the woman's family.

   D. There are 5 people in the woman's family.

2. Which of the following statements is true?

   A. The woman has a dog and a cat at home.

   B. The woman has a dog and 2 cats at home.

   C. The woman has 2 dogs and a cat at home.

   D. The woman has 2 dogs and 2 cats at home.

3. Which of the following statements is true?

   A. The teacher does not have brothers.

   B. The teacher has a younger brother.

   C. The teacher has an older brother.

   D. The teacher has a sister.

4. Which of the following statements is true?

   A. Mr. Wang does not have pets.

   B. Mr. Wang has 3 dogs.

   C. Mr. Wang has 4 cats.

   D. Mr. Wang has a dog and 2 cats.

5. Which of the following statements is true?

   A. There are 3 people in the man's family.

   B. The man has a younger brother.

   C. There are 4 people in the woman's family.

   D. The woman has a younger brother.

I. Listen to the audio recording. Say an appropriate response to each sentence that you hear. Use the space below to make note of your ideas, if necessary.

1. Your response: _____

2. Your response: _____

3. Your response: _____

4. Your response: _____

5. Your response: _____

II. Listen to the audio recording. For each response that you hear, identify and say the appropriate preceding sentence. Use the space below to make note of your ideas, if necessary.

1. Your preceding sentence: _____

2. Your preceding sentence: _____

3. Your preceding sentence: _____

4. Your preceding sentence: _____

5. Your preceding sentence: _____

I. Complete the following Structure Note practices.

Structure Note 2.1: Use 有 to express possession.

> Subject + 有 + Noun Phrase

A. Write the following sentences in Chinese. Record your answers in both pinyin and characters.

		Pinyin	Characters
1.	There are 10 people in her family.	_____	_____
2.	They have 5 cats.	_____	_____
3.	The teacher's family has 3 dogs.	_____	_____
4.	There are many people in China.	_____	_____
5.	There are Chinese people in America.	_____	_____

Structure Note 2.2: Use 没有 to express "not have."

> Subject + 没有 + Noun Phrase

B. Write the following sentences in Chinese. Record your answers in both pinyin and characters.

		Pinyin	Characters
1.	His family does not have dogs.	_____	_____
2.	The teacher's family does not have cats.	_____	_____
3.	Mr. Wang does not have pets.	_____	_____
4.	Mrs Li does not have pets.	_____	_____
5.	There are no cats at Mali's home.	_____	_____

Structure Note 2.3: Use 有没有 to form a "have or not have" question.

$$\boxed{\text{Subject} + 有没有 + \text{Noun Phrase?}}$$

C. Write the following sentences in Chinese. Record your answers in both pinyin and characters.

	Pinyin	Characters
1. Does their family have dogs?		
2. Does the teacher's family have cats?		
3. Does Wang Xiaomei have pets?		
4. Does Li Zhongping have pets?		
5. Are there Chinese people in America?		

Structure Note 2.4: Use 有什么 to ask what one has.

$$\boxed{\text{Subject} + 有 + 什么 + \text{Noun ?}}$$

D. Write the following sentences in Chinese. Record your answers in both pinyin and characters.

	Pinyin	Characters
1. What pets does she have?		
2. What pets does she have at home?		
3. What pets does Xiaomei's family have?		
4. What pets does Zhongping's family have?		
5. What pets does Mr. Wang's family have?		

Structure Note 2.5: Use 的 to indicate possession.

$$\boxed{\text{Noun / Pronoun} + 的 + \text{Noun}}$$

E. Write the following sentences in Chinese. Record your answers in both pinyin and characters.

	Pinyin	Characters
1. His teacher		
2. Their dog		

3. Li Zhongping's father　　_____　　_____

4. Wang Xiaomei's mother　　_____　　_____

5. The teacher's younger sister　　_____　　_____

Structure Note 2.6: Use number + measure word to quantify a noun.

> Number + Measure Word + Noun

F. Write the following sentences in Chinese. Record your answers in both pinyin and characters.

	Pinyin	Characters
1. two dogs	_____	_____
2. five cats	_____	_____
3. three teachers	_____	_____
4. four classmates	_____	_____
5. one teacher (formal)	_____	_____
6. two gentlemen (formal)	_____	_____
7. six ladies (formal)	_____	_____

Structure Note 2.7: Use 几 + measure word to ask how many and number + measure word to answer.

> Subject + Verb + 几 + Measure Word + Noun ?

G. Write the following sentences in Chinese. Record your answers in both pinyin and characters.

	Pinyin	Characters
1. How many people are there in your family?	_____	_____
2. How many people are there in their family?	_____	_____
3. How many dogs does the teacher have?	_____	_____
4. How many cats does Miss Li have?	_____	_____
5. How many teachers are there?	_____	_____

READING COMPREHENSION 2.1

I. Choose the best answers to fill in the blanks.

1. 我有一个 ＿＿＿ 。她十 ＿＿＿ 。
   A. 哥哥⋯⋯九
   B. 弟弟⋯⋯也
   C. 妹妹⋯⋯岁
   D. 弟弟⋯⋯呢

2. ＿＿＿ 老师有两只狗 ＿＿＿ 三只猫。
   A. 他⋯⋯呢
   B. 陈⋯⋯和
   C. 她⋯⋯有
   D. 王⋯⋯叫

3. 我家 ＿＿＿ 六个人。我 ＿＿＿ 是美国人。
   A. 是⋯⋯只
   B. 有⋯⋯们
   C. 没有⋯⋯呢
   D. 是⋯⋯们

4. 我家 ＿＿＿ 宠物。她家 ＿＿＿ 没有宠物。
   A. 没有⋯⋯也
   B. 有⋯⋯很
   C. 多⋯⋯什么
   D. 是⋯⋯是

5. 你家有 ＿＿＿ 个人？你家有 ＿＿＿ 宠物？
   A. 什么⋯⋯几
   B. 哪⋯⋯多
   C. 多⋯⋯哪
   D. 几⋯⋯什么

II. Read the dialogues and answer the following True or False questions.

A.

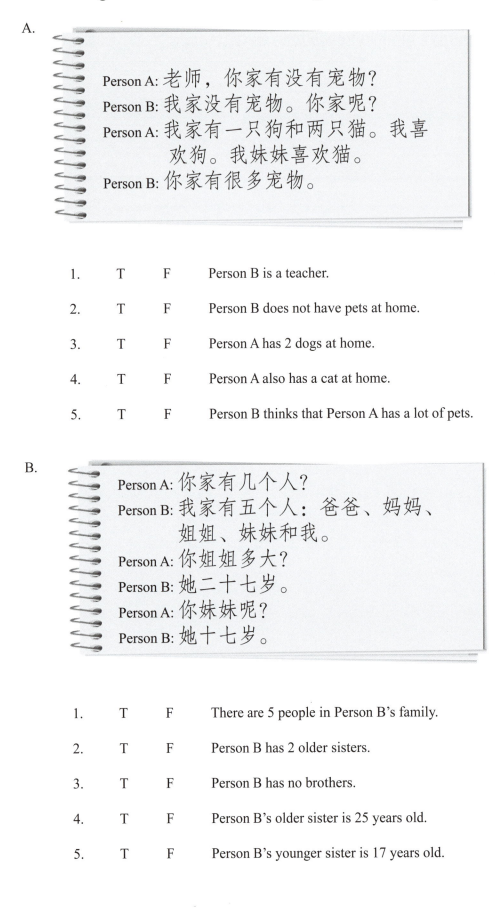

Person A: 老师，你家有没有宠物？

Person B: 我家没有宠物。你家呢？

Person A: 我家有一只狗和两只猫。我喜欢狗。我妹妹喜欢猫。

Person B: 你家有很多宠物。

1.   T   F   Person B is a teacher.

2.   T   F   Person B does not have pets at home.

3.   T   F   Person A has 2 dogs at home.

4.   T   F   Person A also has a cat at home.

5.   T   F   Person B thinks that Person A has a lot of pets.

B.

Person A: 你家有几个人？

Person B: 我家有五个人：爸爸、妈妈、姐姐、妹妹和我。

Person A: 你姐姐多大？

Person B: 她二十七岁。

Person A: 你妹妹呢？

Person B: 她十七岁。

1.   T   F   There are 5 people in Person B's family.

2.   T   F   Person B has 2 older sisters.

3.   T   F   Person B has no brothers.

4.   T   F   Person B's older sister is 25 years old.

5.   T   F   Person B's younger sister is 17 years old.

WRITING PRACTICE 2.1

I. Continue writing your letter to your penpal, using paragraphs and the basic letter format below.

_____ :
(Your penpal's name.)

_____
(Tell him/her about your family.)

_____
(Ask how many people there are in his/her family.)

_____
(Tell him/her about your pets.)

_____
(Ask if he/she has pets at home.)

_____
(Sign your name)

UNIT 2 — LESSON 2

VOCABULARY REVIEW 2.2

I. Mark the correct tones over the pinyin for the vocabulary below. Read the characters aloud as you mark the tones.

1.	男孩	nanhai	8.	谁	shei
2.	工作	gongzuo	9.	说	shuo
3.	汉语	Hanyu	10.	写	xie
4.	汉字	Hanzi	11.	一点儿	yi diǎnr
5.	会	hui	12.	英语	Yingyu
6.	教授	jiaoshou	13.	语言	yuyan
7.	那	na	14.	做	zuo

II. Match the Chinese vocabulary below with the corresponding English meanings.

1. 学生	• •	a. language
2. 咖啡店	• •	b. friend
3. 简单	• •	c. Chinese characters
4. 服务员	• •	d. coffee shop
5. 朋友	• •	e. student
6. 语言	• •	f. simple
7. 汉字	• •	g. waiter

III. Write the pinyin for the professions shown in the pictures. *Read the names of the professions aloud.*

Jobs	Pinyin

IV. Write the pinyin for the languages spoken and written in each country. *Say your answers aloud.*

Country	Spoken language	Written language

CHARACTER WRITING PRACTICE 2.2

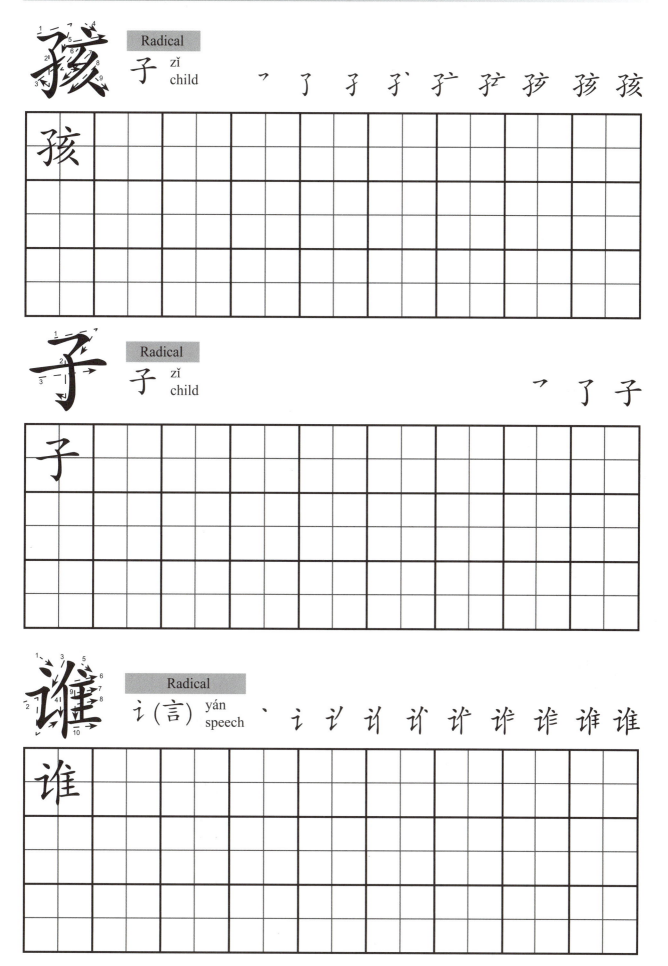

孩

Radical 子 zǐ child

フ了子孑孓孩孩孩孩

子

Radical 子 zǐ child

フ了子

谁

Radical 讠(言) yán speech

丶讠讥讱讲诈诈谁谁

做

Radical
亻(人) rén person

ノ 亻 仁 什 估 估 做 做
做 做

做									

作

Radical
亻(人) rén person

ノ 亻 仁 仁 竹 作 作

作									

言

Radical
言 yán speech

丶 亠 亖 言 言 言 言

言									

Radical

生 shēng
life

ノ ノ ヒ 牛 生

生

Radical

口 kǒu
mouth

ヽ ロ ロ 尸 尸 员 员

员

Radical

人 rén
person

ノ 人 厽 会 会 会

会

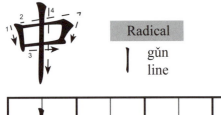

Radical

| gǔn
line

、 口 口 中

中										

Radical

艹(草) cǎo
grass

一 十 艹 艹 节 苎 英 英

英										

Radical

文 wén
script

、 一 ナ 文

文						

还

辶 chuò walk

一 丆 圷 不 还 还 还

还

点

Radical

灬(火) huǒ fire

丨 卜 ﾄ 占 占 点 点 点

点

那

Radical

阝(邑) yì city

刁 コ ヨ 尹 那 那

那

LISTENING COMPREHENSION 2.2

I. Listen to the audio recording and answer the following questions in English or pinyin.

1. A. Tā zuò shénme gōngzuò?

    B. Tā shì nǎ guó rén?

    C. Tā huì shuō shénme yǔyán?

2. A. Tā zuò shénme gōngzuò?

    B. Tā shì nǎ guó rén?

    C. Tā huì shuō shénme yǔyán?

3. A. Tā zuò shénme gōngzuò?

    B. Tā shì nǎ guó rén?

    C. Tā huì shuō shénme yǔyán?

II. Choose the best response to the sentence(s) you hear.

1. A. Wǒ yě huì shuō Yīngyǔ.

    B. Wǒ yě bú huì shuō Yīngyǔ.

    C. Nǐ yě huì shuō Yīngyǔ ma?

    D. Nǐ huì bu huì shuō Yīngyǔ?

2. A. Bú shì wǒ de tóngxué.

    B. Nà shì shéi?

    C. Tā shì wǒ de tóngxué.

    D. Tā jiào shénme míngzi?

3. A. Tā shì shéi?

    B. Shì, tā shì wǒ gēge.

    C. Bú shì. Tā shì wǒ gēge.

    D. Nǐ de dìdi shì shéi?

4. A. Tā shì lǎoshī.

    B. Nǐ shì lǎoshī.

    C. Tā shì bu shì lǎoshī?

    D. Nǐ shì bu shì lǎoshī?

5. A. Wǒ huì xiě yì diǎn Hànzì.

    B. Tā huì shuō Yīngyǔ.

    C. Wǒ huì shuō Zhōngwén.

    D. Nǐ bú huì xiě Hànzì.

III. Choose the best answer for each question, based on each dialogue.

1. Which of the following statements is true?

    A. The woman's father is a teacher.

    B. The woman's father is a businessman.

    C. The man's father is a teacher.

    D. The man's father is a doctor.

2. Which of the following statements is true?

    A. The man can only speak Chinese.

    B. The man can only speak French

    C. The woman can only speak Chinese.

    D. Neither the man nor the woman can speak Chinese.

3. Which of the following statements is true?

    A. The woman's older brother is from China.

    B. The woman's younger brother is from America.

    C. The woman's friend is from America.

    D. The woman's friend is from China.

4. Which of the following statements is true?

    A. The man's mother is a lawyer.

    B. The woman's mother is a lawyer.

    C. Their mothers are both lawyers.

    D. Their mothers are both teachers.

5. Which of the following statements is true?

    A. The teacher can speak a little Chinese.

    B. The teacher cannot write any Chinese characters.

    C. The teacher can write a few Chinese characters.

    D. The teacher can speak and write Chinese.

SPEAKING PRACTICE 2.2

I. Listen to the audio recording. Say aloud an appropriate response to each sentence you hear. Use the space below to make note of your ideas, if necessary.

1. Your response: _____

2. Your response: _____

3. Your response: _____

4. Your response: _____

5. Your response: _____

II. Listen to the audio recording. For each response that you hear, identify and say the appropriate preceding sentence. Use the space below to make note of your ideas, if necessary.

1. Your preceding sentence: _____

2. Your preceding sentence: _____

3. Your preceding sentence: _____

4. Your preceding sentence: _____

5. Your preceding sentence: _____

STRUCTURE REVIEW 2.2

I. Complete the following Structure Note practices.

Structure Note 2.8: Use 这 or 那 to express "this" or "that."

$$\boxed{\text{这 / 那 (+ Number) + Measure Word + Noun}}$$

A. Write the following sentences in Chinese. Record your answers in both pinyin and characters.

		Pinyin	Characters
1.	Who is this?		
2.	Who is that?		
3.	This is Chen Dadong.		
4.	That is Sun Mali.		
5.	This is my mother.		

Structure Note 2.9: Use 谁 to ask "who?"

$$\boxed{\text{Subject + 是 + 谁 ?}}$$

B. Write the following sentences in Chinese. Record your answers in both pinyin and characters.

		Pinyin	Characters
1.	Who is this?		
2.	Who is that?		
3.	Who are they?		
4.	Who is Mr. Wang?		
5.	Who is Ms. Li?		

Structure Note 2.10: Use 还有 to express "also."

$$\boxed{\text{Noun + 、 + Noun + 还有 + Noun}}$$

C. Write the following sentences in Chinese. Record your answers in both pinyin and characters.

	Pinyin	Characters
1. Mother, father, older brother	_____	_____
2. English, Chinese, French	_____	_____
3. Lawyer, teacher, student	_____	_____
4. China, America, Canada	_____	_____
5. Two boys, one girl, one cat	_____	_____

Structure Note 2.11: Use 会 to state what one knows how to do.

Subject + 会 + Verb Phrase

D. Write the following sentences in Chinese. Record your answers in both pinyin and characters.

	Pinyin	Characters
1. I can speak English.	_____	_____
2. They can write English.	_____	_____
3. We can speak French.	_____	_____
4. My older sister can write French.	_____	_____
5. My older brother can speak Chinese.	_____	_____

Structure Note 2.12: Use 会不会 to ask whether or not one knows how to do something.

Subject + 会不会 + Verb Phrase ?

E. Write the following sentences in Chinese. Record your answers in both pinyin and characters.

	Pinyin	Characters
1. Can you speak English?	_____	_____
2. Can they speak French?	_____	_____
3. Can the teacher speak Chinese?	_____	_____
4. Can Miss Wang write English?	_____	_____
5. Can Mr. Li write Chinese characters?	_____	_____

Structure Note 2.13: Use 只 to express "only."

$$\boxed{\text{Subject Phrase} + \text{只} + \text{Verb Phrase}}$$

F. Write the following sentences in Chinese. Record your answers in both pinyin and characters.

	Pinyin	Characters
1. There are only two people in his family.		
2. I only have one younger brother.		
3. She only has a younger sister.		
4. Mrs. Li only has a dog.		
5. The teacher only has a cat.		

I. Below is an application form for enrolling in a language class. Identify the languages mentioned in this application form.

广州外教网语言交流申请表
(http://www.teachingd.com)

广州市天河区中山大道190号骏景花园骏怡轩G502

电话.: +86-20-80556499   +86-20-31320707

电邮: teachingd@126.com

Photo

基本信息

中文名字:_____   英文名字:_____

　　性别:_____　　　　　　生日:_____

　　电话:_____　　　　　　手机:_____

　　邮箱:_____　　　　　　地址:_____

工作年限:_____   目前状态: 学生　　就业

毕业院校:_____   所学专业:_____

语言信息
母语:　　　　　　　第二语言:

期望练习的语言	☐英语　　　　　☐法语　☐西班牙语
	☐意大利语　　　☐德语　☐荷兰语　☐其他

II. Choose the best answers to fill in the blanks.

1. 我 (i)____ 爸爸五十六岁。(ii)____ 是教授。他是中 (iii)____ 人。他只会说汉 (iv)____。

(i) A. 呢　　　　(ii) A. 不　　　　(iii) A. 文　　　　(iv) A. 文
　　B. 是　　　　　　B. 只　　　　　　B. 国　　　　　　B. 国
　　C. 有　　　　　　C. 他　　　　　　C. 语　　　　　　C. 语
　　D. None　　　　　D. 她　　　　　　D. 岁　　　　　　D. 岁

2. 她哥哥 (i)____ 美国人，可是他会 (ii)____ 汉语。他也会 (iii)____ 汉字。他是 (iv)____ 老师。

(i) A. 呢　　　　(ii) A. 不　　　　(iii) A. 叫　　　　(iv) A. 中文
　　B. 是　　　　　　B. 只　　　　　　B. 写　　　　　　B. 中国
　　C. 有　　　　　　C. 说　　　　　　C. 只　　　　　　C. 医生
　　D. None　　　　　D. 叫　　　　　　D. 都　　　　　　D. 学生

III. Read the passage and answer the following True or False questions.

我家有四个人：爸爸、妈妈、哥哥和我。我们是美国人。我爸爸五十九岁。他是语言老师。我妈妈五十五岁。她也是语言老师。他们会说很多语言：中文、英语和法语。我和我的哥哥只会说英语。我哥哥三十岁。他是律师。我是学生。

1. T F The author is the youngest in his family.

2. T F The author's family is from America.

3. T F The author's parents are both older than 60.

4. T F The author's parents are both language teachers.

5. T F The author's parents can speak Chinese, English and Japanese.

6. T F The author can only speak English.

7. T F The author's older brother is a businessman.

8. T F The author is a student.

WRITING PRACTICE 2.2

I. Continue writing your letter to your penpal, using paragraphs and the letter format below.

_____ :

(Your penpal's name)

_____ 。

(Tell him/her about your family makeup.)

_____ 。

(Tell him/her what kind of work your family members do.)

_____ 。

(Tell him/her what languages you can speak.)

_____ 。

(Ask him/her what languages he/she can speak.)

_____

(Sign your name)

VOCABULARY REVIEW 3.1

I. Mark the correct tones over the pinyin for the vocabulary below. Read the characters aloud as you mark the tones.

1.	星期	xingqi	11.	吧	ba	
2.	足球	zuqiu	12.	现在	xianzai	
3.	比赛	bisai	13.	差不多	chabuduo	
4.	去	qu	14.	分	fen	
5.	什么	shenme	15.	对不起	duibuqi	
6.	时候	shihou	16.	没关系	mei guanxi	
7.	晚上	wanshang	17.	看	kan	
8.	开始	kaishi	18.	走	zou	
9.	点	dian	19.	刻	ke	
10.	半	ban	20.	时间	shijian	

II. Match the Chinese vocabulary below with the corresponding English meanings.

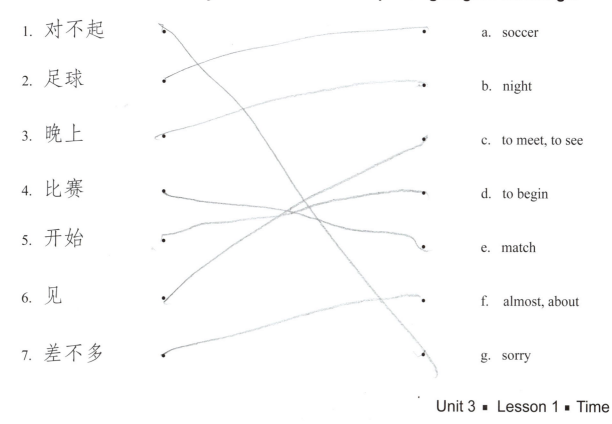

1. 对不起   a. soccer

2. 足球   b. night

3. 晚上   c. to meet, to see

4. 比赛   d. to begin

5. 开始   e. match

6. 见   f. almost, about

7. 差不多   g. sorry

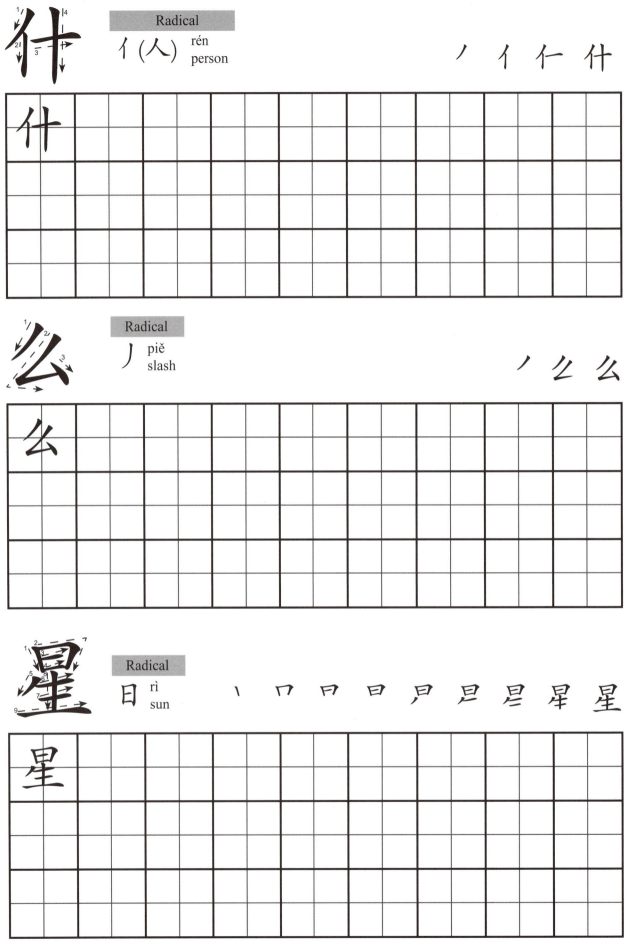

Radical

亻(人) rén person

ノ 亻 仁 什

什

Radical

ノ piě slash

ノ 厶 么

么

Radical

日 rì sun

丶 丿 冂 曰 日 尸 早 星 星

星

期

月 yuè
moon

一 十 艹 艹 甘 甘 其 其 期

期 期 期

期

时

Radical
日 rì
sun

丨 冂 冂 日 日一 时 时

时

上

Radical
一 yī
one

丨 卜 上

上

钟

钅(金) jīn gold 　ノ　ケ　ヒ　ゟ　钅　钟　钟　钟　钟

钟											

半

、 diǎn dot 　　　　　丶　丷　ソ　ゾ　半

半											

在

土 tǔ earth 　　　　一　ナ　才　右　在　在

在											

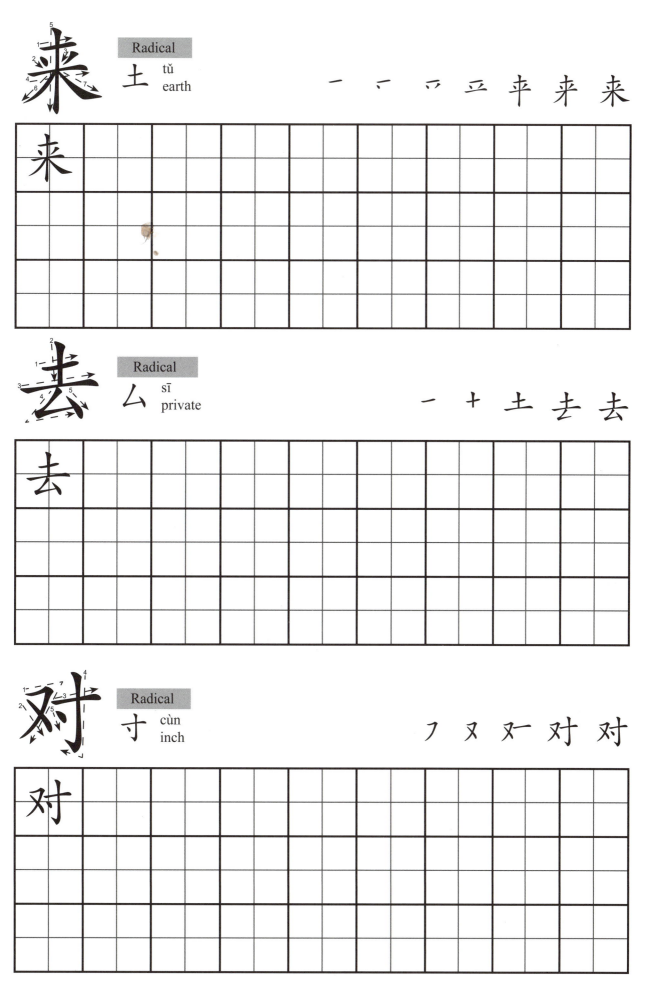

 **Radical**

走 zǒu
walk

一 十 土 キ キ キ 走 走 起

起 起

起										

 Radical

丌 gǒng
hands
joined

一 二 于 开

开										

始 **Radical**

女 nǚ
woman

〈 〈 女 女 女 始 始 始

始										

I. Listen to the audio recording and choose the best answer for the options below.

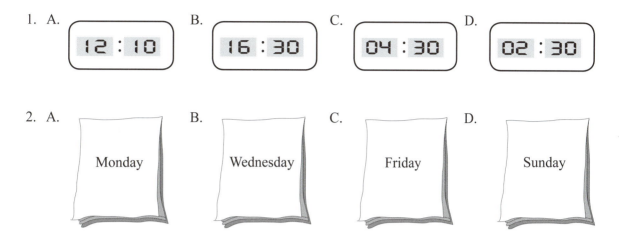

1. A. `12:10`   B. `16:30`   C. `04:30`   D. `02:30`

2. A. Monday   B. Wednesday   C. Friday   D. Sunday

II. Listen to the audio recording and answer the questions.

1. What day is the soccer game?

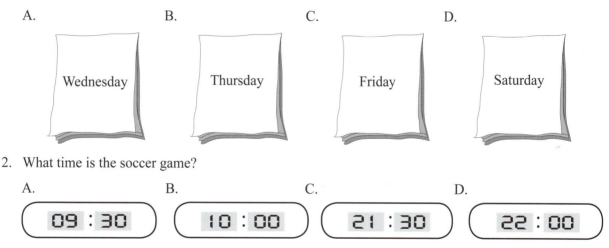

   A. Wednesday   B. Thursday   C. Friday   D. Saturday

2. What time is the soccer game?

   A. `09:30`   B. `10:00`   C. `21:30`   D. `22:00`

3. Which of the statements is NOT true?

   A. There is a soccer game this week.

   B. The woman asks what day of the week the soccer game is on.

   C. The man asks the woman if she will go to the soccer game.

   D. They will meet each other at 9:30 a.m.

III. Listen to the audio recording and answer the question.

1. Which of the statements is NOT true?

   A. The boy and girl will meet each other.

   B. The boy asks the girl to meet him at 6:30 p.m.

   C. The boy asks the girl what time they should meet.

   D. The girl suggests they meet at 6:45 p.m.

I. Listen to the audio recording. Say aloud an appropriate response to each sentence you hear. Use the space below to make note of your ideas, if necessary.

1. Your Response: _____

2. Your Response: _____

3. Your Response: _____

4. Your Response: _____

5. Your Response: _____

II. Using the information given, make an audio recording in which you tell your friend about a soccer game you plan to go to. Ask if he or she will go, too. Use the space below to make note of your ideas, if necessary.

Date: Friday, October 22

Time: 4:30 p.m.

I. Complete the following Structure Note practices.

Structure Note 3.1: Use 会 to indicate the possibility of an action taking place in the future.

> Subject + 会 + Verb

A. Mark which of the following sentences indicate the possibility of a future action using 会.

( ) 1. 你会去咖啡店吗?

( ) 2. 你会写汉字吗?

( ) 3. 她晚上会来吗?

( ) 4. 你会说英语吗?

( ) 5. 我下个星期会去加拿大。

Structure Note 3.2: Use 什么时候 to ask "when."

> Subject + 什么时候 + Verb Phrase ?

B. Make sentences by using 什么时候 with the given words.

1. 你 / 来我家?   你什么时候来我家?

2. 你们 / 工作?   你们什么时候工作

3. 爸爸 / 去咖啡店?   爸爸什么时候去啡咖啡店

4. 足球比赛 / 开始?   足球比赛什么时候开始

5. 他 / 去美国?   他什么候时候去美国?

Structure Note 3.3: Use 星期几 to ask "what day of the week" and 星期 + number to state the day of the week.

> 星期几 / 星期 + Number

C. Write the following sentences in Chinese using the correct time expressions.

1. What day is today? 今天星期几？

2. What day is the football match? _____

3. I will go to a soccer game on Tuesday. _____

4. What day of the week will you go to Canada? _____

5. She will go to China next Friday. _____

Structure Note 3.4: Use 几点 to discuss time.

> Subject + 几点 + Verb

D. Write the following sentences in Chinese using 几点.

1. What time does the game start? 比赛几点开始？

2. What time do you go to school? 你几点去学

3. What time is it now? 现在几点

4. What time will we meet? 我们几点

5. What time will Mr. Chen come? _____

Structure Note 3.5: Use 差不多 to express "almost."

> 差不多 + Number

E. Rewrite the following sentences using 差不多.

1. 孙老师五十岁。_____

2. 我弟弟十三岁。_____

3. 现在八点一刻。_____

4. 现在十二点半。_____

5. 现在七点四十五分。_____

Structure Note 3.6: Use 还没（有）to express "not yet" or "still have not."

> Subject + 还没（有）+ Verb

F. Rewrite the sentences below using 还没（有）.

1. 我去加拿大。_____

2. 他去学校。_____

3. 玛丽开始学中文。_____

4. 足球比赛开始。_____

5. 大东来。_____

Structure Note 3.7: Use 吧 to make a suggestion.

> Sentence + 吧

G. Transform the sentences below into suggestions using 吧.

1. 我们走。 我_____

2. 我们开始。_____

3. 晚上七点见。_____

I. Read the passages and answer the following True or False questions.

A.

> 这个星期五下午四点有足球比赛。大东、祥安和玛丽会去看。大东说："我们三点半见吧！"祥安说："我差不多三点去。"大东说："没关系，三点比赛还没开始。"

1.　　T　　F　　Dadong, Xiang'an and Mali are going to a soccer game on Friday.

2.　　T　　F　　The soccer game will start at 3 o'clock.

3.　　T　　F　　They will meet at 4 o'clock.

4.　　T　　F　　Xiang'an will get there at about 3:45 p.m.

5.　　T　　F　　Xiang'an will be late for the soccer game.

B.

> 陈大东是加拿大人，他差不多二十岁，他会说中文、英语和法语。星期六，他在咖啡店工作。星期天下午，他看足球比赛。

1.　　T　　F　　Chen Dadong is Chinese.

2.　　T　　F　　Chen Dadong is about 20 years old.

3.　　T　　F　　Chen Dadong can speak Mandarin, English, and French.

4.　　T　　F　　Chen Dadong works full time at a coffee shop.

5.　　T　　F　　Chen Dadong watches football on Sunday afternoons.

WRITING PRACTICE 3.1

I. Write the information on the poster to announce the date / time / place of a school soccer game.

DATE: _____

TIME: _____

PLACE: _____

II. Write an e-mail in which you invite your friend to the school soccer game. Use the information in the poster and the words in the word bank below.

| 足球 | 比赛 | 点 | 星期 | 见 | 开始 |

| Sender | |
| Subject | |

VOCABULARY REVIEW 3.2

I. Mark the correct tones above the pinyin for the vocabulary below. Read the characters aloud as you mark the tones.

1.	生日	shengri	9.	高兴	gaoxing
2.	月	yue	10.	大家	dajia
3.	号	hao	11.	吃	chi
4.	十月	shi yue	12.	蛋糕	dangao
5.	明天	mingtian	13.	送	song
6.	派对	paidui	14.	礼物	liwu
7.	生日快乐	shengri kuaile	15.	祝	zhu
8.	都	dou	16.	真	zhen

II. Fill in the gaps in the sequences below to create complete chronological progressions.

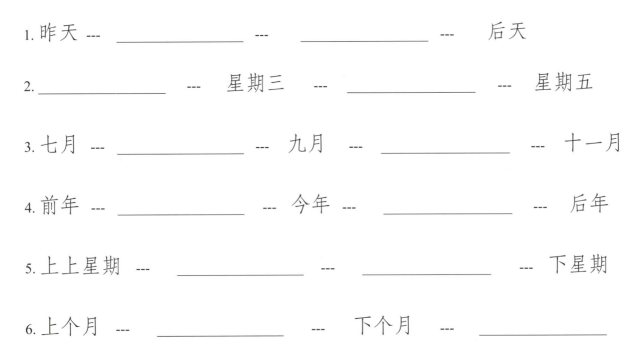

1. 昨天 --- _____ --- _____ --- 后天

2. _____ --- 星期三 --- _____ --- 星期五

3. 七月 --- _____ --- 九月 --- _____ --- 十一月

4. 前年 --- _____ --- 今年 --- _____ --- 后年

5. 上上星期 --- _____ --- _____ --- 下星期

6. 上个月 --- _____ --- 下个月 --- _____

CHARACTER WRITING PRACTICE 3.2

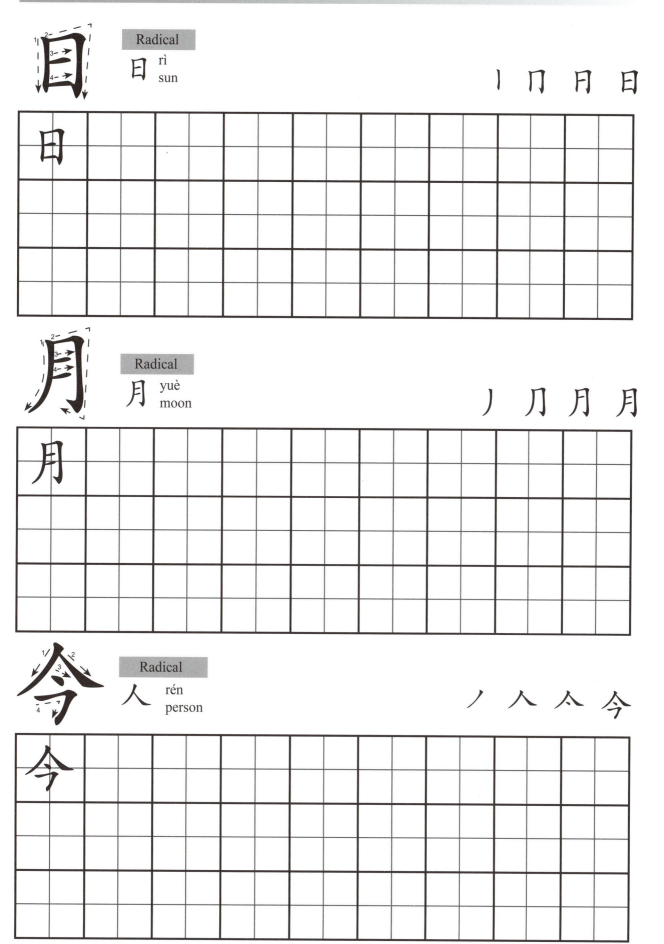

Radical

日 rì
sun

丨 冂 月 日

Radical

月 yuè
moon

丿 冂 月 月

Radical

人 rén
person

丿 人 亼 今

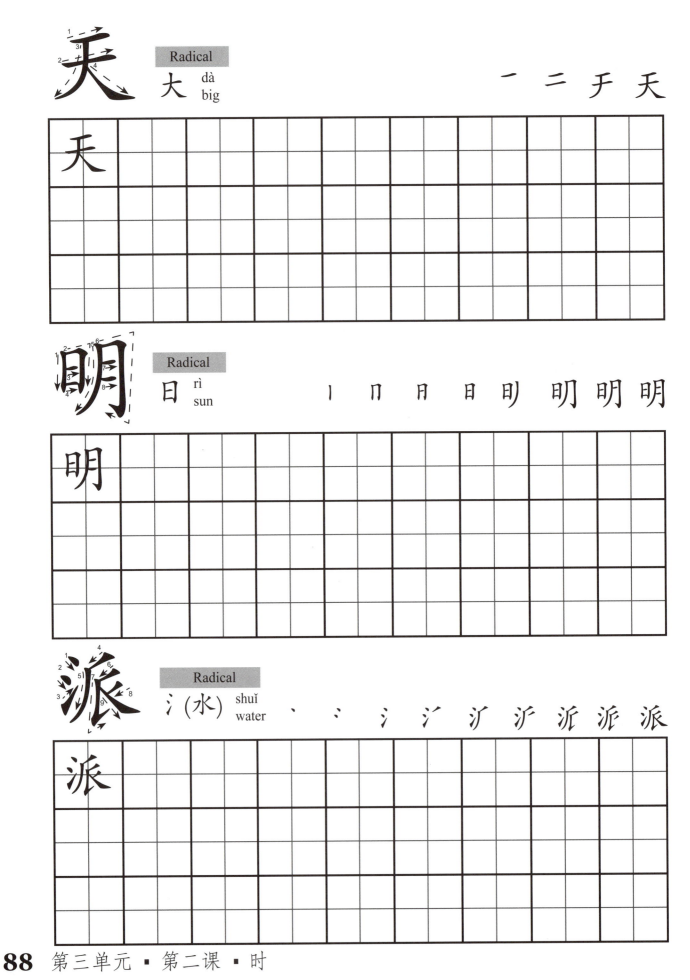

天

大 dà big

一 二 チ 天

天

明

Radical

日 rì sun

丨 冂 月 日 日 明 明 明

明

派

Radical

氵(水) shuǐ water

、 丶 氵 汀 汇 汇 浉 派 派

派

昨

Radical

日 rì sun

丨 丨 冂 月 日 日ˊ 旷 昨 昨 昨

昨

快

Radical

忄(心) xīn heart

丶 丷 忄 忄 忙 快 快

快

乐

Radical

丿 piě slash

丿 丆 乐 乐 乐

乐

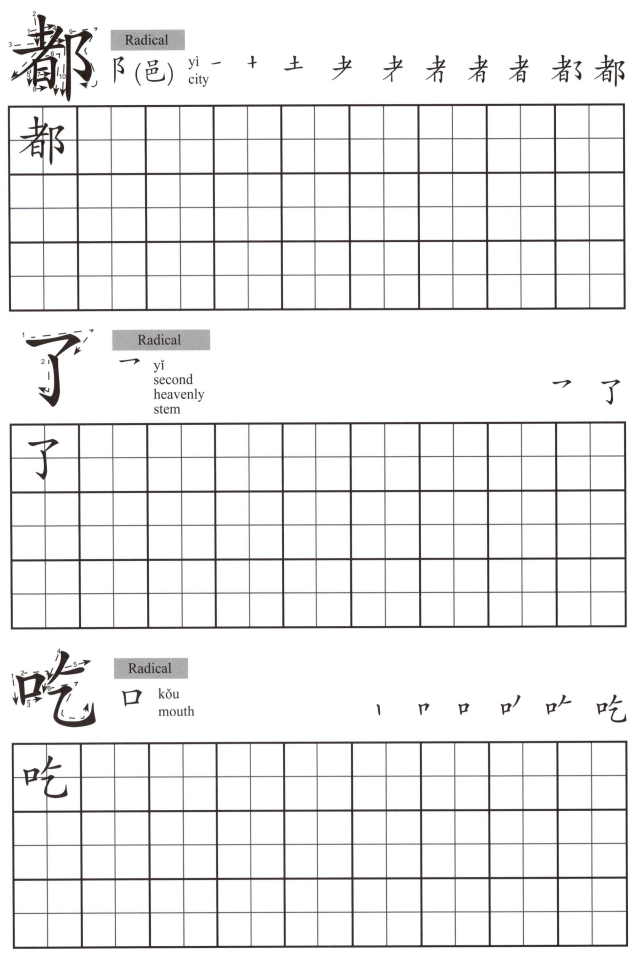

都   **Radical**
阝(邑) yì — + 土 耂 耂 者 者 者 者 都 都
city

了   **Radical**
一 yǐ
second
heavenly
stem
     一 了

吃   **Radical**
口 kǒu
mouth
     丶 丨 口 口 口 吃

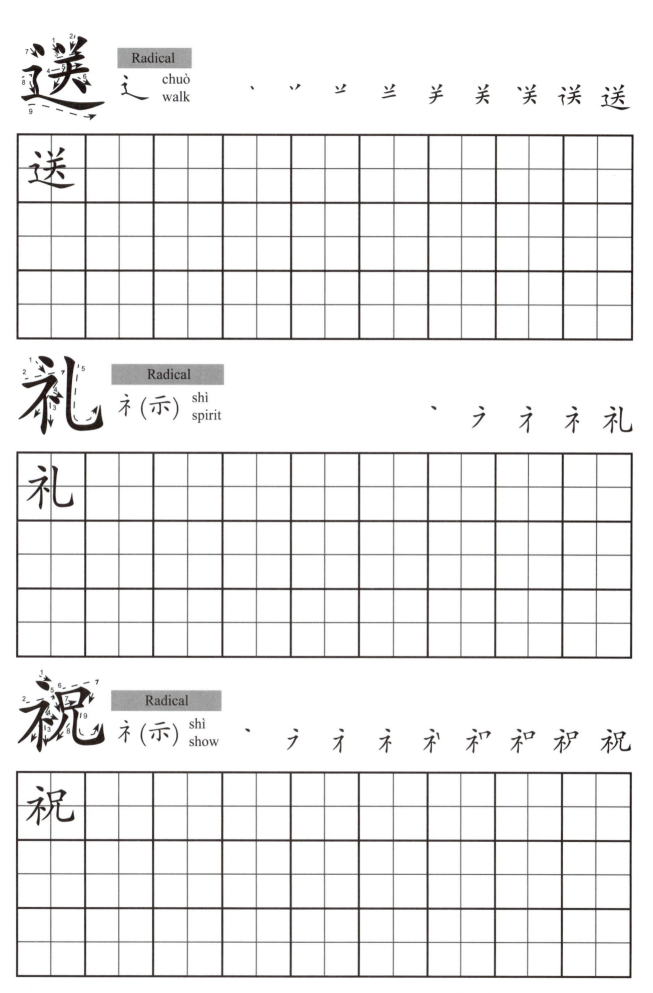

送 | Radical | 辶 chuò walk | 丶 丶 丷 丷 兰 关 关 关 误 送
送

礼 | Radical | 礻 (示) shì spirit | 丶 ㇋ ㇋ 礻 礼
礼

祝 | Radical | 礻 (示) shì show | 丶 ㇋ ㇋ 礻 礻 礻 初 初 祝
祝

I. Choose the picture that best illustrates what you hear.

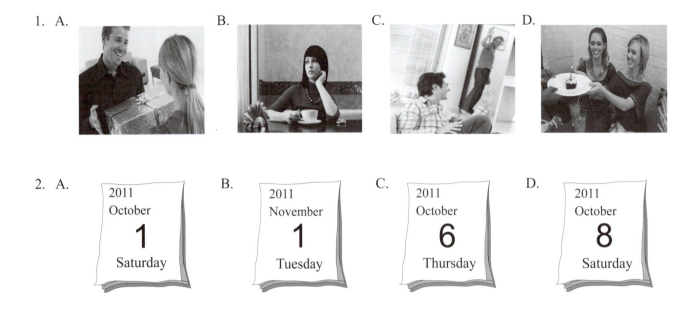

1. A.   B.   C.   D.

2. A.   2011 October 1 Saturday   B.   2011 November 1 Tuesday   C.   2011 October 6 Thursday   D.   2011 October 8 Saturday

II. Choose the best response to the sentence(s) you hear.

1. A. 是吗？
   B. 谢谢你！
   C. 祝你生日快乐！
   D. 没关系！

2. A. 明天是我的生日。
   B. 我是中文老师。
   C. 我不是咖啡店的服务员。
   D. 我会去你的生日派对。

3. A. 他的生日是十月十五号。
   B. 我明天会去他的生日派对。
   C. 今天是妹妹的生日。
   D. 他的生日是明天。

III. Answer the question based on the dialogue.

1. Which of the following statements is NOT true?
   A. Today is Mali's birthday.
   B. Today is October 2nd.
   C. Tomorrow is October 3rd.
   D. The man and the woman will get her a birthday present.

IV. Answer the questions based on the dialogue.

1. What is the nationality of the man?
   A. Canadian
   B. Chinese
   C. British
   D. American

2. What is the age of the man?
   A. 18
   B. 20
   C. 21
   D. 31

3. Which of the following statements is true?
   A. The woman's birthday is on May 31st.
   B. The man is Wang Xiaomei's brother.
   C. The man is the woman's classmate.
   D. Wang Xiaomei is the man's classmate.

I. Listen to the audio recording. Say an appropriate response to each sentence you hear. Use the space below to make note of your ideas, if necessary.

1. Your Response: _____

2. Your Response: _____

3. Your Response: _____

4. Your Response: _____

5. Your Response: _____

II. Imagine that Friday is your Chinese teacher's 50th birthday. Make an audio recording in which you organize a birthday party for her/him. Use the space below to make note of your ideas, if necessary.

星期五	中文老师	五十岁	生日派对
吃	蛋糕	送	生日礼物
祝	生日快乐	高兴	同学

STRUCTURE REVIEW 3.2

I. Complete the following Structure Note practices.

Structure Note 3.8: Use 几 to ask "what month" and "what day."

> Subject (+ 是) + 几月几号？

A. Answer the questions below in complete sentences.

1. 你的生日是几月几号？ _____

2. 明天是几月几号？ _____

3. 圣诞节 (Shèngdànjié: Christmas) 是几月几号？ _____

4. 情人节 (Qíngrénjié: Valentine's day) 是几月几号？ _____

5. 下星期六是几月几号？ _____

Structure Note 3.9: Use 都 to mean "both" or "all."

> Subject + 都 + Verb Phrase

B. Rewrite the following sentences using 都.

1. 我们来了！ _____

2. 他们是美国人。 _____

3. 你们不会说中文吗？ _____

4. 他们是我的朋友。 _____

5. 大东和玛丽是服务员。 _____

Structure Note 3.10: Use 了 to indicate a change of state or stituation.

> Sentence + 了

C. Change the following sentences to indicate a change of state.

1. 我没有工作。 _____

2. 他不是我的朋友。 _____

3. 比赛开始。 _____

4. 大东来。 _____

5. 我有一只猫。 _____

Structure 3.11: Use the verb 送 in the context of gift giving.

> Subject + 送 + Recipient + Object

D. Make complete sentences using 送 and the given words.

1. 这是 / 爸爸 / 我的 / 生日礼物。 _____

2. 这是 / 我 / 你的 / 咖啡。 _____

3. 他 / 玛丽 / 一份 / 礼物。 _____

4. (Create your own sentence) _____

5. (Create your own sentence) _____

Structure 3.12: Use 的 to modify nouns.

> Modifier + 的 + Noun

E. Create sentences using the given words, adding 的 to modify the appropriate noun.

1. 那 / 是 / 陈老师 / 写 / 字。

_____

2. 这 / 是 / 我 / 送 / 生日礼物。

_____

3. 这 / 是 / 我 / 朋友 / 写 / 汉字。

_____

4. 这 / 是 / 她 / 妈妈 / 做 / 蛋糕。

_____

5. 那 / 是 / 学校 / 咖啡店。

_____

I. Fill in the blanks and answer the questions in the following section.

都	礼物	蛋糕	派对	生日	很

上星期六是玛丽的 (i) _____，朋友们

(ii) _____来她的生日 (iii) _____，玛丽

(iv) _____高兴。大家送她生日 (v) _____，

中平送她咖啡，小美送她 (vi) _____。

Based on the passage above, answer the following True or False questions.

1.　T　F　Mali's birthday is next Saturday.

2.　T　F　Mali's friends came to her birthday.

3.　T　F　Zhongping gave Mali a cake as a gift.

4.　T　F　Xiaomei brought some coffee to the party.

5.　T　F　Mali was very happy that her friends came to the party.

II. Answer the questions in Chinese based on Xiang'an's calendar.

八月

星期天	星期一	星期二	星期三	星期四	星期五	星期六
		1	2	3	4	5
6	7	8 中国父亲节 Chinese Father's Day	9	10	11	12
13 足球比赛	14	15	16	17	18	19 玛丽的派对
20	21	22	23	24	25	26 妈妈的生日
27	28	29 返校日 (fǎnxiào rì) Back to school	30	31		

1. What day of the week is the first day of August?

_____

2. What day of the week is Mali's party?

_____

3. How many Thursdays are in this month?

_____

4. What date is Xiang'an's mother's birthday?

_____

5. What day of the week is the first day of September?

_____

WRITING PRACTICE 3.2

I. Type the following sentences in Chinese and answer the questions.

1. What date is your birthday?

2. It is Tuesday, September 23.

3. Tomorrow is my 20th birthday. Will you come to my birthday party?

4. I was so happy that all of you came to my birthday party.

5. This is the birthday gift I am giving to you.

II. Make a list of the birthdays of your family members, relatives, and friends.

Name（名字）	Birthday (月／日)	Age (岁)
爸爸		
妈妈		

III. Complete the birthday party invitation card below.

十八　　十月十五日　　生日　　下午五点
生日派对　　三　　咖啡店　　蛋糕

下个星期 ＿＿＿＿是我 ＿＿＿＿岁＿＿＿

的 ＿＿＿＿。那天会有我的 ＿＿＿＿＿＿＿。

Date:　　　　　　　　　　Time:

Place:　　　　　　　　　Food provided:

VOCABULARY REVIEW 4.1

I. Mark the correct tones above the pinyin for the vocabulary below. Read the characters aloud as you mark the tones.

1.	欢迎	huanying	7.	烧鸡	shaoji
2.	服务员	fúwùyuan	8.	青菜	qingcai
3.	请坐	qing zuo	9.	酸辣汤	Suanlatang
4.	菜单	caidan	10.	饭馆	fanguan
5.	喜欢	xihuan	11.	点菜	dian cai
6.	饺子	jiaozi			

II. Match the Chinese vocabulary below with the corresponding pictures.

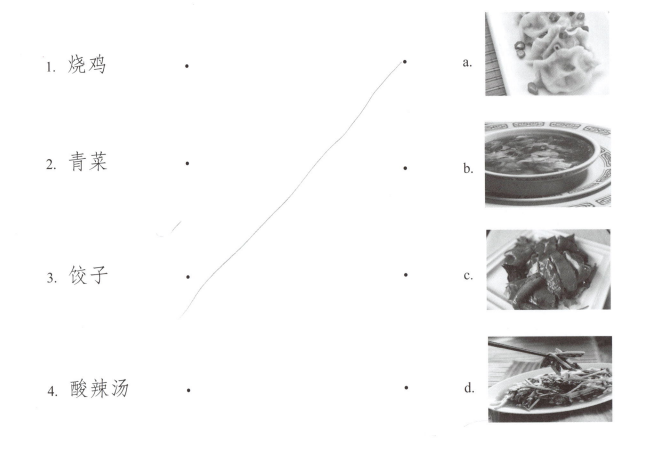

1. 烧鸡 •

2. 青菜 •

3. 饺子 •

4. 酸辣汤 •

• a.

• b.

• c.

• d.

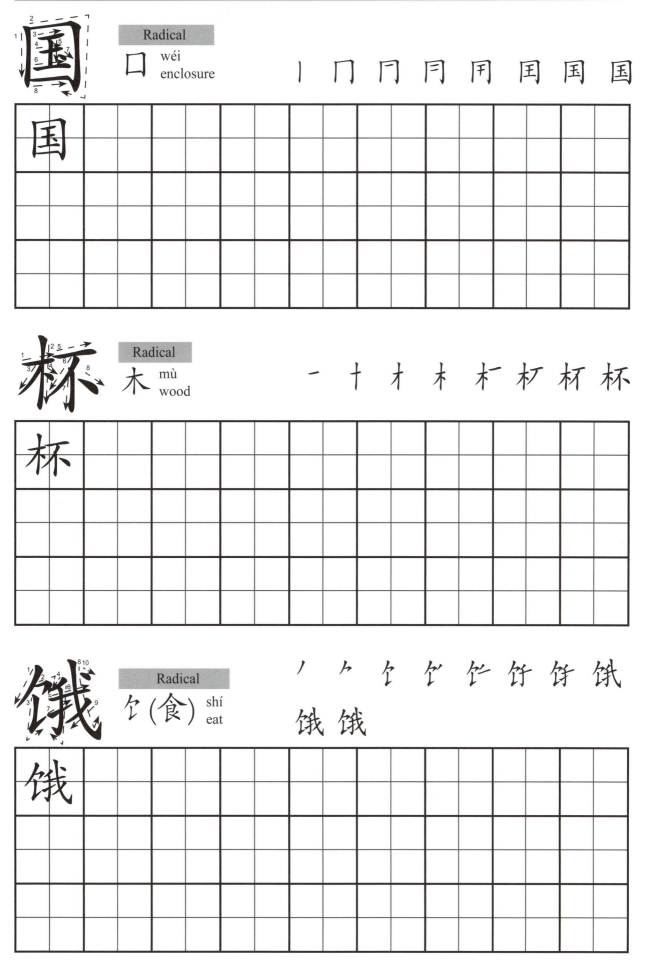

国　Radical　口 wéi enclosure

丨 冂 冂 冃 用 囯 国 国

杯　Radical　木 mù wood

一 十 才 木 杧 杧 杯 杯

饿　Radical　饣(食) shí eat

丿 亇 亇 饣 饣 饣 饿 饿

饿 饿

光 儿 rén person

光 **Radical**

丶 丷 业 光 光

位 亻(人) rén person

亻 亻 亻 位 位 位 位

位 **Radical**

坐 土 tǔ earth

丿 人 人人 从 从 坐 坐

坐 **Radical**

想 **Radical** 心 xīn heart 一 十 才 木 村 机 相 相 相 相 想 想 想

想								

喝 **Radical** 口 kǒu mouth 丨 口 口 叩 叩 吗 吗 吗 喝 喝 喝

喝								

给 **Radical** 纟(丝) sī silk 乙 纟 纟 纟 纟 纟 给 给 给

给								

新 **Radical** 斤 jīn axe

、 ᐟ 亠 六 立 立 辛 辛 亲
亲 新 新 新

份 **Radical** 亻(人) rén person

ノ 亻 仆 仏 份 份

青 **Radical** 青 qīng blue

一 二 キ 主 丰 青 青 青

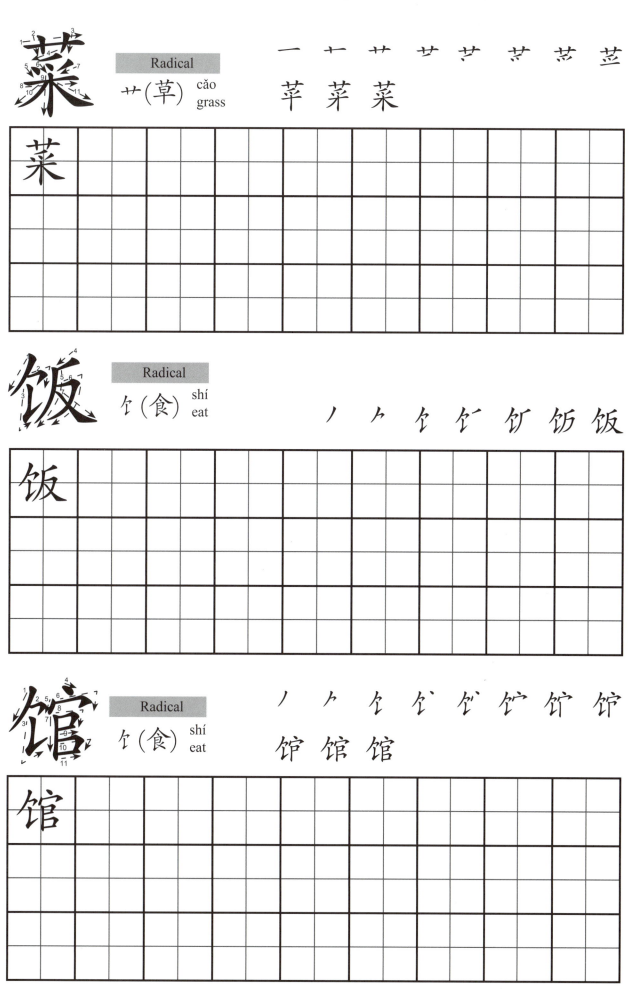

菜

Radical

艹 (草) cǎo grass

一　十　艹　艹　艹　艹　艹

苹　苹　菜

饭

Radical

饣 (食) shí eat

丿　勹　饣　饣　饣　饭　饭

馆

Radical

饣 (食) shí eat

丿　勹　饣　饣　饣　饣　饣　饣

馆　馆　馆

I. Choose the picture that best illustrates what you hear.

1.

A.   B.   C.   D.

2.

A.   B.   C.   D.

II. Listen to the recording and answer the questions.

1. What food does the woman want to have?
   A. American
   B. Chinese
   C. Italian
   D. Japanese

2. What food will they order?
   A. Dumplings
   B. Spicy beef
   C. Dumplings and Vegetables
   D. Dumplings and Hot and Sour Soup

3. Which of the following statements is NOT true?
   A. The man and the woman eat dinner together.
   B. The woman wants to have Chinese food.
   C. The man suggests they have dumplings for dinner.
   D. The woman wants to have Hot and Sour Soup instead of dumplings.

III. Listen to the recording and answer the questions.

1. Which of the following statements is NOT true?
   A. The waitress seats the customers at a table.
   B. The waitress asks what drink they want to order.
   C. The restaurant does not offer tea.
   D. The customer orders three cups of tea.

I. Listen to the audio recording. Say an appropriate response to each sentence you hear. Use the space below to make note of your ideas, if necessary.

1. Your Response: _____

2. Your Response: _____

3. Your Response: _____

4. Your Response: _____

5. Your Response: _____

II. Imagine you are with a large group of friends in a restaurant. Using the menu below, make an audio recording in which you order dishes for everybody. You should order at least two items from each section. Remember to use the correct measue words.

菜单	菜单
★饮料 Drink	**★汤** Soup
咖啡 Coffee	酸辣汤 Hot & Sour Soup
红茶 (Hóng chá) Black Tea	青菜汤 Vegetable Soup
绿茶 (Lǜ chá) Green Tea	鸡汤 Chicken Soup
可乐 (Kělè) Cola	
	★主菜 Entrée
★点心 Appetizer	烧鸡 Roast Chicken
	咖喱鸡 (Gālí jī) Curry Chicken
饺子 Dumplings	鸡炒饭 (Jī chǎofàn) Chicken Fried Rice
小笼包 (Xiǎo lóng bāo) Steamed Pork Buns	蛋炒饭 (Dàn chǎofàn) Egg Fried Rice
八宝饭 (Bā bǎo fàn) Eight Treasure Rice	上海菜饭 (Shànghǎi cài fàn) Shanghai Vegetable Rice

I. Complete the following Structure Note practices.

Structure Note 4.1: Use 想 to indicate a desired action.

> Subject + 想 + Verb + Object

A. Add 想 to the following sentences to indicate preferences.

1. 王老师喝咖啡。 _____

2. 你们吃饺子吗？ _____

3. 我看足球比赛。 _____

4. 他喝茶。 _____

5. (Create your own sentence) _____

Structure Note 4.2: Use 给 to mean "to give."

> Subject + 给 + Recipient + Object

B. Make sentences using 给 and the given words.

1. 他 / 我 / 一份 / 生日 / 礼物

_____

2. 请 / 我们 / 菜单

_____

3. 服务员 / 我们 / 三杯 / 茶

_____

4. 请 / 我 / 一份 / 青菜

_____

5. 玛丽 / 中平 / 一杯 / 咖啡

Structure Note 4.3: Use 喜欢 to express liking something or someone.

> Subject + 喜欢 + Verb Phrase / Noun

C. Transform the sentences below by adding 喜欢 to the appropriate place.

1. 我吃中国菜。 _____

2. 王小姐喝咖啡。 _____

3. 大东看足球比赛。 _____

4. (Create your own sentence) _____

5. (Create your own sentence) _____

Structure Note 4.4: Use Verb + 不 + Verb with two-character verbs to form affirmative-negative questions.

> 2-Character Verb + 不 + 2-Character Verb

> 1st Character of 2-Character Verb + 不 + 2-Character Verb

D. Change the following questions into questions using the "Verb 不 Verb" pattern.

1. 她是你的妹妹吗?

_____

2. 你喜欢喝酸辣汤吗?

_____

3. 大东喜欢猫吗?

_____

4. 你想吃中国菜吗?

_____

5. (Create your own sentence.)

_____

Structure Note 4.5: Use 那 (么) to mean "Well then" or "In that case."

$$\boxed{那（么）+ \text{Statement / Question}}$$

E. Respond to the following prompts using 那 (么).

1. A: 我不想去学校。

   B: _____

2. A: 她不会说英语。

   B: _____

3. A: 我想喝酸辣汤。

   B: _____

4. A: 我不想吃美国菜。

   B: _____

5. A: 大东不来我的生日派对。

   B: _____

Structure Note 4.6: Use 好 + Verb to form a compound adjective.

$$\boxed{好 + \text{Verb}}$$

F. Add 好 to the correct place in the sentences below.

1. 妈妈做的烧鸡 / 很 / 吃。_____

2. 这个字 / 不 / 写。_____

3. 这家的咖啡 / 很 / 喝。_____

4. 她写的汉字 / 很 / 看。_____

5. 你的生日蛋糕 / 很 / 吃。_____

I. Choose the best answers to fill in the blanks and answer the following questions.

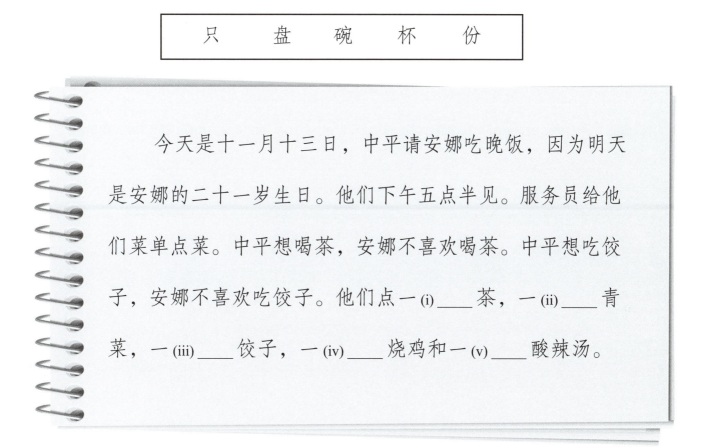

| 只 | 盘 | 碗 | 杯 | 份 |

今天是十一月十三日，中平请安娜吃晚饭，因为明天是安娜的二十一岁生日。他们下午五点半见。服务员给他们菜单点菜。中平想喝茶，安娜不喜欢喝茶。中平想吃饺子，安娜不喜欢吃饺子。他们点一(i)＿＿茶，一(ii)＿＿青菜，一(iii)＿＿饺子，一(iv)＿＿烧鸡和一(v)＿＿酸辣汤。

Answer the following questions in Chinese.

1. Why did Zhongping treat Anna to dinner?

_____

2. What date is Anna's birthday?

_____

3. How old is Anna?

_____

4. What time did they meet?

_____

5. What did Zhongping want to eat?

_____

6. Does Anna like to drink tea?

_____

7. What kind of restaurant do you think they went to?

_____

II. Choose the best answers to fill in the blanks and answer the following questions.

酸辣汤	茶	饺子	中国菜	青菜

陈大东是加拿大人，他二十岁，是孙玛丽的同学。

他和孙玛丽去饭馆吃 (i) _____，他不饿，只点一杯

(ii) _____ 和一份 (iii) _____。孙玛丽点一盘

(iv) _____ 和一碗 (v) _____。

Answer the following True or False questions on the basis of the passage above.

1.　T　F　Chen Dadong is American.

2.　T　F　Sun Mali and Chen Dadong are classmates.

3.　T　F　Chen Dadong and Sun Mali go to eat Chinese food.

4.　T　F　Mali orders dumplings and Hot and Sour Soup.

5.　T　F　Chen Dadong is not hungry, so he only orders a cup of coffee.

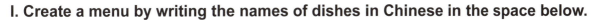

WRITING PRACTICE 4.1

I. Create a menu by writing the names of dishes in Chinese in the space below.

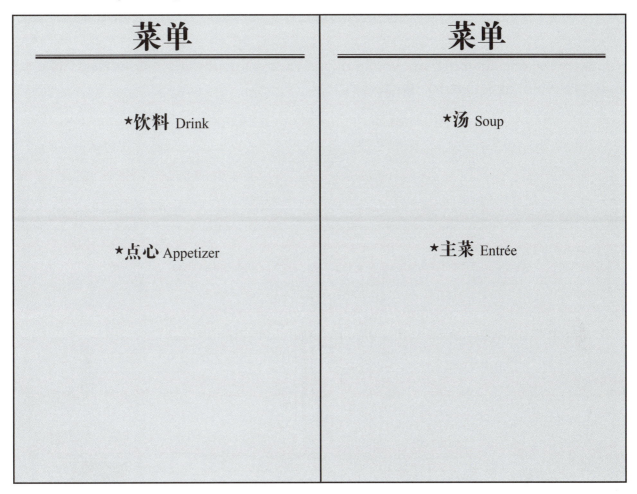

菜单

★饮料 Drink

★点心 Appetizer

菜单

★汤 Soup

★主菜 Entrée

II. Based on the menu above, write a paragraph or conversation using the given words in the space below.

请问　是不是　好不好　喜欢不喜欢　那

UNIT 4 – LESSON 2

VOCABULARY REVIEW 4.2

I. Mark the correct tones above the pinyin for the vocabulary below. Read the characters aloud as you mark the tones.

1.	太咸	tai xian	6.	筷子	kuaizi	
2.	一碗	yi wan	7.	试一下	shi yi xia	
3.	不错	bucuo	8.	很简单	hen jiandan	
4.	酸辣	suanla	9.	吃饱	chi bao	
5.	米饭	mifan	10.	我教你	wo jiao ni	

II. Match the flavors below with the corresponding pictures.

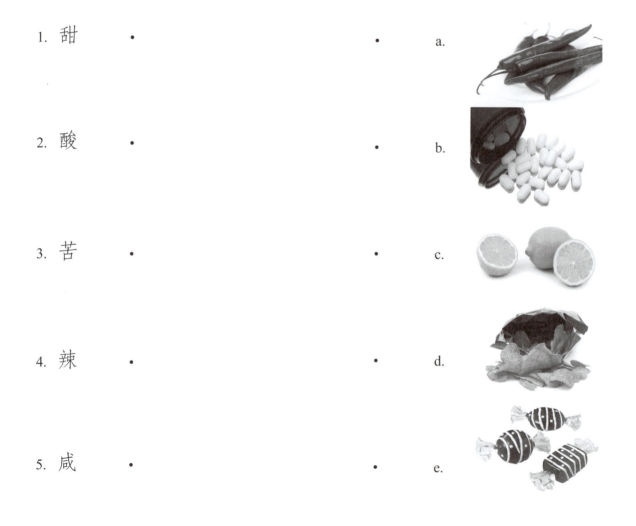

1. 甜   •

2. 酸   •

3. 苦   •

4. 辣   •

5. 咸   •

a.

b.

c.

d.

e.

CHARACTER WRITING PRACTICE 4.2

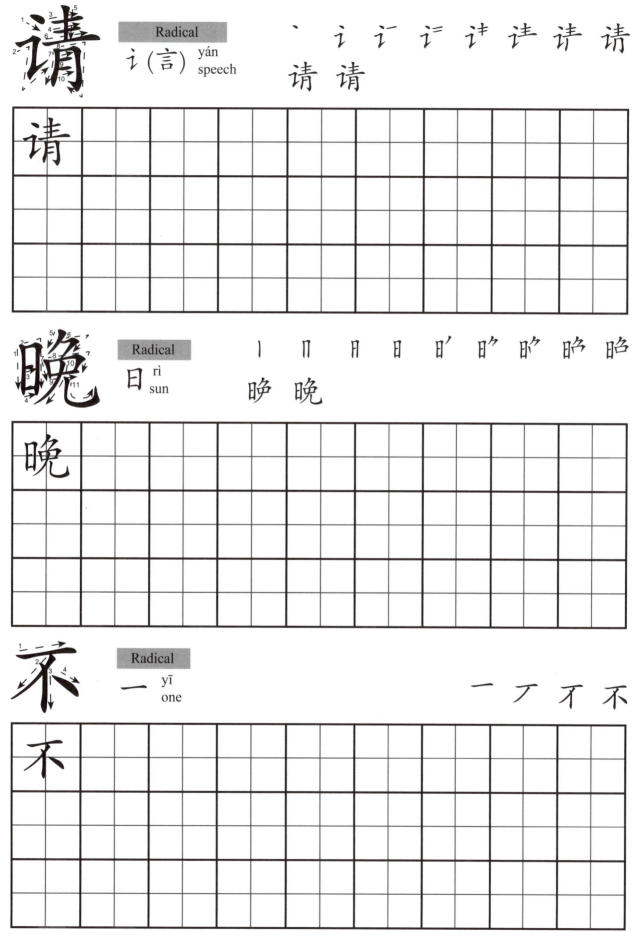

Radical
讠(言) yán
speech

丶 讠 讠 订 计 请 请 请
请 请

晚

Radical
日 rì
sun

丨 冂 冃 日 日' 日' 肜 晔 晚
晔 晚

不

Radical
一 yī
one

一 丁 不 不

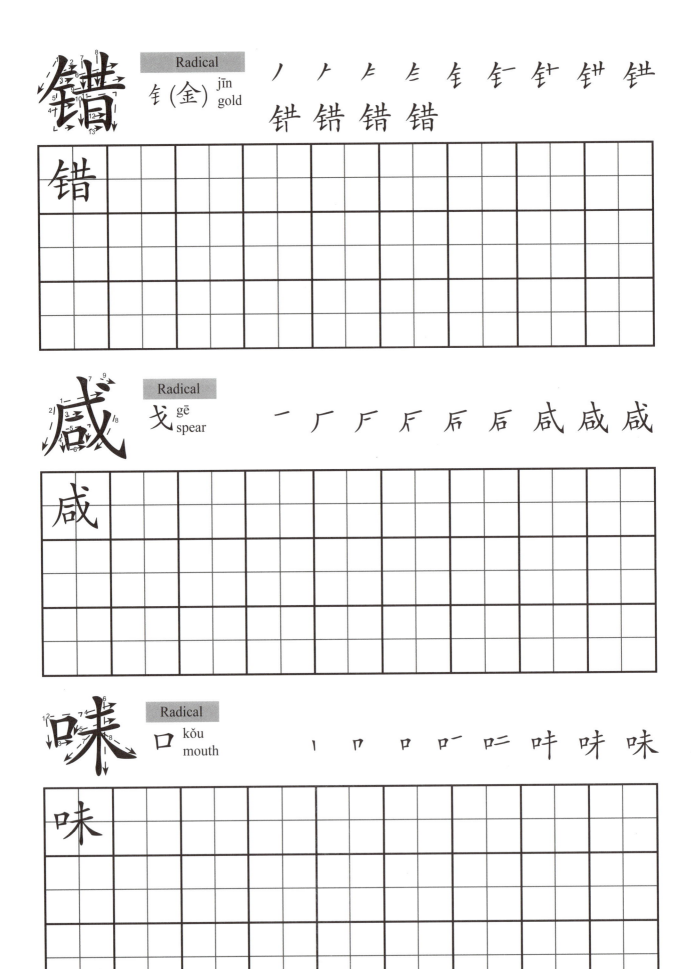

错

Radical

钅(金) jīn
gold

丿 𠂊 𠂉 钅 钅 钅 钔 钟 钟
钟 错 错 错

错

咸

Radical

戈 gē
spear

一 厂 厂 厂 厂 咸 咸 咸 咸

咸

味

Radical

口 kǒu
mouth

丨 卩 口 口 口 呋 呋 味

味

道

Radical
辶 chuò walk

丶 丶 丷 丷 艹 首 首 首 首 道

道 道

道										

怎

Radical
心 xīn heart

丿 𠂆 乍 乍 乍 怎 怎 怎

怎										

太

Radical
大 dà big

一 ナ 大 太

太										

要

Radical
西 yà
cover

一 一 一 一 一 西 西 要 要 要

要

因

Radical
囗 wéi
enclosure

丨 冂 冂 因 因 因

因

为

Radical
丶 diǎn
dot

丶 丿 为 为

为

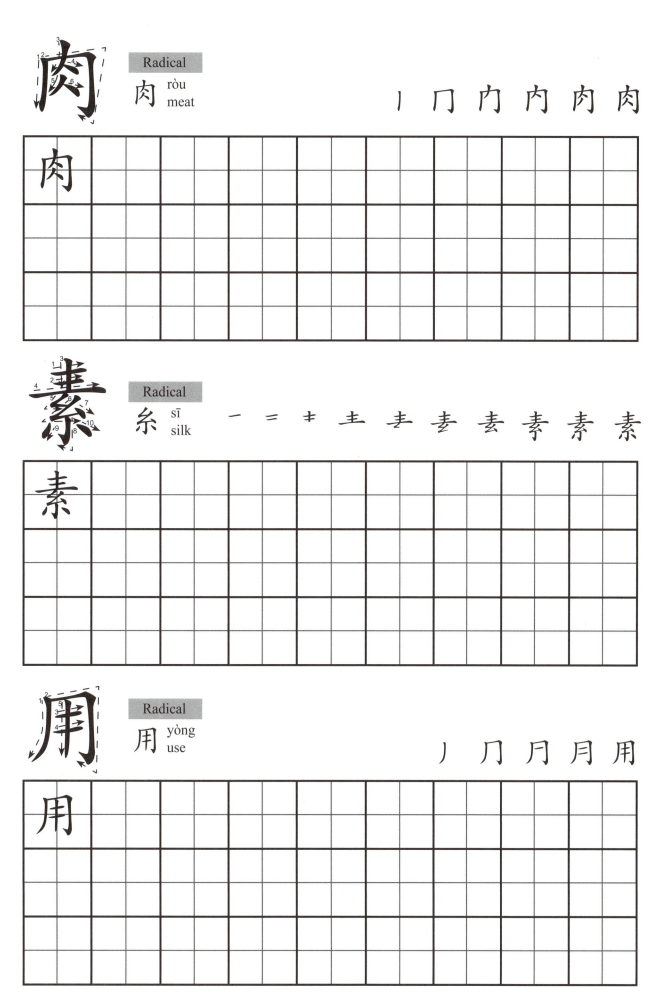

肉 ròu meat

丿 冂 内 内 肉 肉

素 sī silk

一 二 キ 主 丰 麦 麦 素 素 素

用 yòng use

丿 冂 月 月 用

I. Choose the picture that best illustrates what you hear.

1. A.   B.   C.   D.

2. A.   B.   C.   D.

II. Choose the best response to the sentence(s) you hear.

1. A. 谢谢你！   C. 我不喜欢吃辣。
   B. 我喜欢吃中国菜。   D. 我吃素。

2. A. 我不吃肉。   C. 太咸了。
   B. 我想吃青菜。   D. 请给我一杯茶。

III. Answer the question based on the dialogue.

1. Which of the following statements is NOT true?
   A. The woman doesn't know how to use chopsticks.
   B. She doesn't know how to use a knife and fork.
   C. The man tries to help the woman use chopsticks.
   D. The woman thinks it is not difficult to learn how to use chopsticks.

IV. Answer the questions based on the dialogue.

1. Where do you think the dialogue happened?
   A. At school   C. On the street
   B. At a restaurant   D. At a party

2. What does the woman like to eat?
   A. Chicken   C. Dumplings
   B. Hot and Sour Soup D. Rice

3. Which of the following statements is true?
   A. The woman complains about the restaurant.
   B. The man asks for the woman's opinion on the dumplings.
   C. The woman insists the man try the Hot and Sour Soup.
   D. The man asks for a beverage.

SPEAKING PRACTICE 4.2

I. Listen to the audio recording. Say an appropriate response to each sentence you hear. Use the space below to make note of your ideas, if necessary.

1. Your Response: _____

2. Your Response: _____

3. Your Response: _____

4. Your Response: _____

5. Your Response: _____

II. Make an audio recording in which you call a friend and offer to take him/her out to dinner. Tell him/her the reason why you want to pay for the dinner. Ask your friend's preferences and talk about what dishes you like. Use the space below to make note of your ideas, if necessary.

I. Complete the following Structure Note practices.

Structure Note 4.7: Use 怎么样 to ask for an opinion of something.

$$\boxed{\text{Subject} + 怎么样？}$$

A. Write the following sentences in Chinese using 怎么样.

1. How is this restaurant ?

_____

2. How was the party yesterday?

_____

3. How is your job?

_____

4. How does the birthday cake taste?

_____

5. How was the competition last Monday?

_____

Structure Note 4.8: Use 太……了 to describe an exaggerated attribute.

$$\boxed{太 + \text{Adjective} + 了}$$

B. Change the following sentences by substituting 很 for 太……了.

1. 这碗酸辣汤很辣。

_____

2. 你的中文很好。

_____

3. 这盘青菜很咸。

_____

4. 妈妈做的菜很好吃。

_____

5. 这杯茶很好喝。

_____

Structure Note 4.9: Use 要 to indicate desire.

> Subject + 要 + Noun / Verb Phrase

C. Create sentences by using the "Subject + 要 + Noun/Verb Phrase" pattern and the given words.

1. (看足球比赛) _____

2. (一盘饺子) _____

3. (一只猫) _____

4. (去咖啡店) _____

5. (三杯茶) _____

Structure Note 4.10: Use 为什么 and 因为 to ask questions and give explanations respectively.

> Subject + 为什么 + Verb Phrase

> 为什么 + Subject + Verb Phrase

> 因为 + Supporting Reason

D. Complete the following dialogues using the 为什么 and 因为 patterns.

1. A: _____

   B: 因为我不会。

2. A: 他为什么不说中文？

   B: _____

3. A: _____

   B: 因为她吃素。

4. A: _____

   B: _____

5. A: _____

   B: _____

Strucutre Note 4.11: Use 一下 to express the brevity of an action.

> Subject + Verb + 一下 (+ Object)

E. Add 一下 to an appropriate place in the sentences below.

1. 请看我们的菜单。

   _____

2. 请坐。

   _____

3. 看我的狗。

   _____

4. 试我们的烧鸡吧!

   _____

5. 请说你的名字。

   _____

I. Read the passage and answer the questions below.

中平吃素。
小美不喜欢吃米饭，也不吃辣的。
安娜不喜欢喝茶。
玛丽只喜欢吃辣的。

According to the passage, what should each person order? Choose the appropriate food or drink in Chinese.

| Hot and Sour Soup | Rice | Coffee | Tea | Dumplings | Vegetables |

1. Zhongping _____

2. Xiaomei _____

3. Anna _____

4. Mali _____

II. Read the dialogue and answer the following true or false questions.

大东：酸辣汤很好喝！我喜欢吃辣。
玛丽：烧鸡也不错。中平，青菜的味道怎么样?
中平：太咸了！我要叫一杯茶。
大东：中平，你为什么只吃青菜，不吃肉?
中平：因为我吃素。
玛丽：你吃一碗米饭吧！
中平：谢谢！我吃饱了！

1.　　T　　F　　Dadong likes the spicy food.

2.　　T　　F　　Zhongping is a vegetarian.

3.　　T　　F　　Mali thinks the chicken is good.

4.　　T　　F　　Zhongping is full.

5.　　T　　F　　Zhongping wants a cup of tea because the soup is too salty.

I. Write or type sentences in Chinese according to the given phrases and pictures.

1. 很好吃

2. 怎么样

3. 好不好

4. 会不会

5. 为什么

II. Write or type sentences in Chinese to describe the taste of the dishes below and whether or not you like them.

1.

2.

3.

UNIT 5 – LESSON 1

VOCABULARY REVIEW 5.1

I. Mark the correct tones above the pinyin for the vocabulary below. Read the characters aloud as you mark the tones.

1.	介绍	jieshao	9.	图书馆	tushuguan
2.	同屋	tongwu	10.	对面	duimian
3.	认识	renshi	11.	看书	kan shu
4.	校园	xiaoyuan	12.	运动	yundong
5.	大学	daxue	13.	可以	keyi
6.	餐厅	canting	14.	一起	yiqi
7.	公寓	gongyu	15.	当然	dangran
8.	里面	limian	16.	回头见	huitou jian

II. Match the Chinese vocabulary below with the corresponding English meanings.

1. 图书馆 •   • a. dining hall

2. 校内 •   • b. on-campus

3. 餐厅 •   • c. gym

4. 大学 •   • d. classroom

5. 健身房 •   • e. off-campus

6. 教室 •   • f. library

7. 校外 •   • g. college, university

高 gāo tall

Radical

、　亠　亠　古　卞　戸　高　高　高　高

高

兴

Radical

八 bā eight

、　丷　丷　ソ　屵　兴　兴

兴

认

Radical

讠(言) yán speech

、　讠　认　认

认

识

Radical

讠(言) yán
speech

丶 讠 记 识 识 识

识

住

Radical

亻(人) rén
person

丿 亻 彳 亻 仁 住 住

住

校

Radical

木 mù
wood

一 十 才 木 朳 杧 栌 栌 栌 校

校

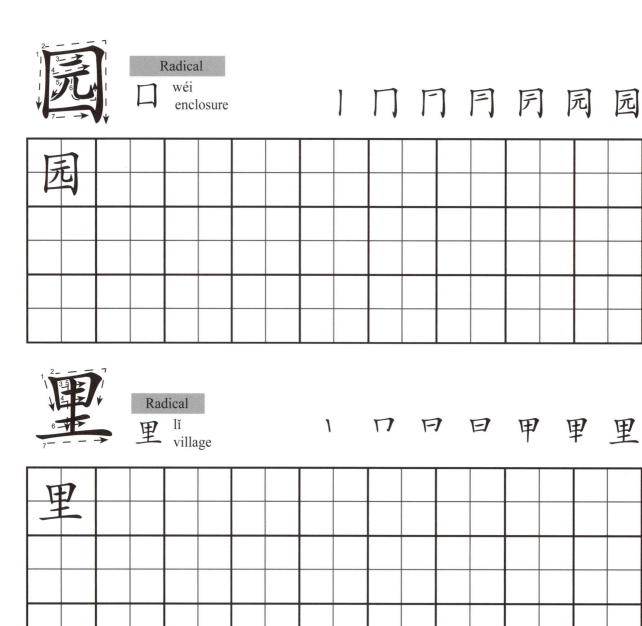

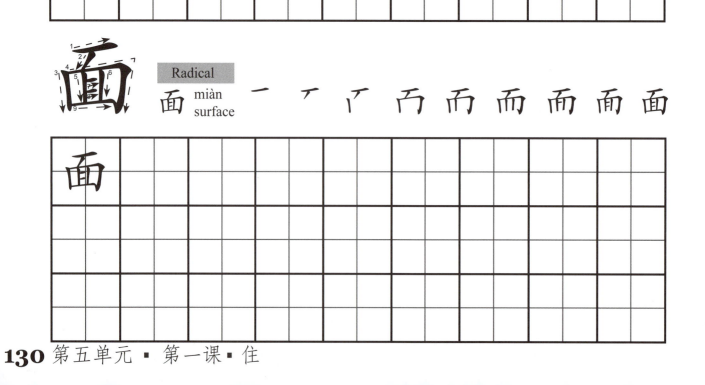

第五单元 · 第一课 · 住

Radical

之 chuò walk

一 二 テ 云 运 运 运

Radical

目 mù eye

一 二 三 チ 矛 看 看 看 看

Radical

乙 yǐ second heavenly stem

フ ㄓ 书 书

跟

Radical

足 zú foot

丶 冖 口 口 尸 尸 足 足 趴

趴 趴 跟 跟

跟										

当

Radical

ヨ jì snout

丶 丷 丷 当 当 当

当										

然

Radical

灬(火) huǒ fire

丿 勹 夕 夕 夗 妖 然

然 然 然 然

然										

LISTENING COMPREHENSION 5.1

I. Listen to the recording and answering the following True or False questions.

( ) 1. Wang Xiaomei is a new student.

( ) 2. Wang Xiaomei lives on campus.

( ) 3. Chen Dadong lives near Wang Xiaomei.

( ) 4. Wang Xiaomei lives across from the Chinese restaurant.

II. Listen to the recording and answering the following True or False questions.

( ) 1. The woman is going to the library.

( ) 2. The man is going to a restaurant.

( ) 3. The man invites the woman to go with him.

( ) 4. The woman agrees to let the man come with her.

III. Listen to the recording and answering the following True or False questions.

( ) 1. Today is the man's birthday.

( ) 2. Chen Dadong is the man's roommate.

( ) 3. There will be a birthday party.

( ) 4. The restaurant is next to the library.

SPEAKING PRACTICE 5.1

I. A new student asks you how to get to various facilities on campus. Make an audio recording in which you answer his/her questions in complete sentences according to the map provided. Use the space below to make note of your ideas, if necessary.

1. Where is the library?_____

2. Where is the cafeteria? _____

3. Where is the gym?_____

4. Where is the coffee shop?_____

5. Where is the Chinese restaurant? _____

STRUCTURE REVIEW 5.1

I. Complete the following Structure Note practices.

Structure Note 5.1: Use 在 to indicate location.

> Subject (+ 不) + 在 + Location (+ 的) + Place Word

A. Add 在,的 and 面 or 边 into the appropriate places below to create complete sentences.

1. 我家 / 咖啡店 / 后 _____

2. 餐厅 / 图书馆 / 对 _____

3. 陈大东 / 教室 / 外 _____

4. 健身房 / 咖啡店 / 前 _____

5. 公寓 / 校园 / 里 _____

Structure Note 5.2: Use 在 as a verb complement.

> Subject (+ 不) + Verb + 在 + Location

B. Write the following sentences in Chinese using the pattern above.

1. Where do you live? _____

2. I live across from the Chinese restaurant. _____

3. My friend lives in America. _____

4. She does not live in France. _____

5. Do you live on campus? _____

Structure Note 5.3: Use 哪里 to ask "where."

> Subject + 在 + 哪里

> Subject + Verb + 在 + 哪里

> Subject + Verb + 哪里

C. Write the sentences below in Chinese using 在哪里.

1. Where is the restaurant?_____

2. Where is Chen Dadong?_____

3. Where does he live?_____

4. Where do the students sit? _____

5. Where will she go tomorrow? _____

Structure Note 5.4: Use 要 to talk about future events.

$$\boxed{\text{Subject} + 要 + \text{Verb Phrase}}$$

D. Answer the questions using 要 / 不会.

1. 你今年会去中国吗？

(positive answer):_____

(negative answer): _____

2. 你们会去他的生日派对吗？

(positive answer):_____

(negative answer): _____

3. 他会跟谁一起来？（他的爸爸妈妈）

_____

4. A: 你要去哪儿？

B: _____

5. A:你什么时候要去加拿大？

B: _____

Structure Note 5.5: Use 跟……一起 to express doing things together.

> Subject 1 + 跟 + Subject 2 (+ 一起) + Verb Phrase

E. Create sentences using the given vocabulary.

1. 我，爸爸，妈妈，住。（不跟／一起）

_____

2. 我，昨天，大东，去，看，足球比赛。（跟／一起）

_____

3. 你，要，谁，去，法国？（跟／一起）

_____

4. 学生们，孙老师，学，中文。（跟）

_____

5. 祥安，小美，去，健身房。（跟／一起）

_____

Structure Note 5.6: Use 可以 to express permission.

> Subject + 可以 + Verb Phrase

F. Write the following sentences in Chinese using 可以.

1. Can I use your Chinese textbook?_____

2. Can we order now? _____

3. Can I eat this cake? _____

4. Can I go to the library with you tomorrow? _____

5. Can we go to the birthday party on Wednesday?_____

I. Read the passage and answer the questions.

大东跟祥安是室友，他们住在校园里的宿舍，在餐厅的对面。他们都喜欢运动。大东星期六和星期天工作，祥安星期一上午和星期三晚上去看足球比赛。星期五下午他们一起去健身房。

1. What is the relationship between Dadong and Xiang'an?
   A. Roommates
   B. Brothers
   C. Friends
   D. Coworkers

2. Where do Dadong and Xiang'an live?
   A. Next to the cafeteria on the campus
   B. Off-campus
   C. Across from the cafeteria on the campus
   D. In front of the library

3. Which of the following statements is NOT true?
   A. Both Dadong and Xiang'an like exercising.
   B. Xiang'an works on Monday and Wednesday.
   C. Dadong has a part-time job on the weekend.
   D. They go to the gym together on Friday afternoons.

II. Read the passage and answer the questions.

祥安会说汉语，也会写一点汉字。十一月二十四号是祥安的二十岁生日，朋友们都来他的生日派对。晚上祥安跟他的朋友们去中国饭馆吃饭。玛丽送他一个大蛋糕，大家都很高兴。

1. What date is Xiang'an's birthday?
   A. September 24
   B. October 20
   C. November 20
   D. November 24

2. What statement about Xiang'an is NOT true?
   A. He is 20 years old.
   B. He cannot speak Chinese.
   C. He can write a little bit of Chinese.
   D. In the evening, he went to a Chinese restaurant.

3. What did Mali do for Xiang'an's birthday?
   A. Bought him dinner
   B. Took him to a party
   C. Gave him a cake
   D. Went to see a football match with him

I. Look at the campus map below. Explain in 3 – 5 sentences where the labeled buildings are in relation to each other.

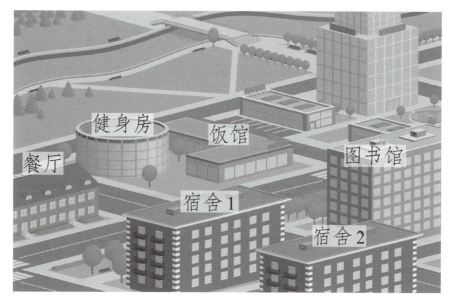

_____

_____

_____

_____

_____

II. Xiaomei is a freshman. She is trying to decide whether to live on or off-campus. Write her an e-mail and tell her the pros and cons of living on or off-campus.

Sender	
Subject	

VOCABULARY REVIEW 5.2

I. Mark the correct tones above the pinyin for the vocabulary below. Read the characters aloud as you mark the tones.

1.	宿舍	sushe	6.	里面	limian
2.	卧室	woshi	7.	床	chuang
3.	可能	keneng	8.	电视	dianshi
4.	书桌	shuzhuo	9.	沙发	shafa
5.	帮	bang	10.	课本	keben

II. Using the words in the box, describe where the cat is in the following pictures.

上面　下面　里面　外面　前面　后面

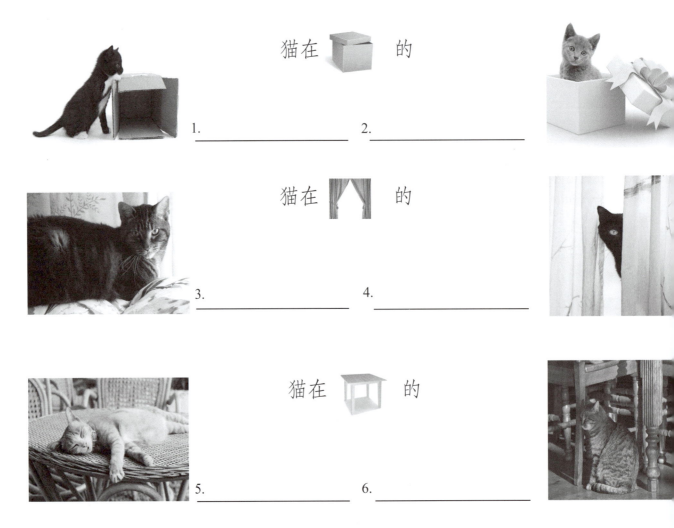

猫在 ⬜ 的

1. _____ 2. _____

猫在 🎭 的

3. _____ 4. _____

猫在 🪑 的

5. _____ 6. _____

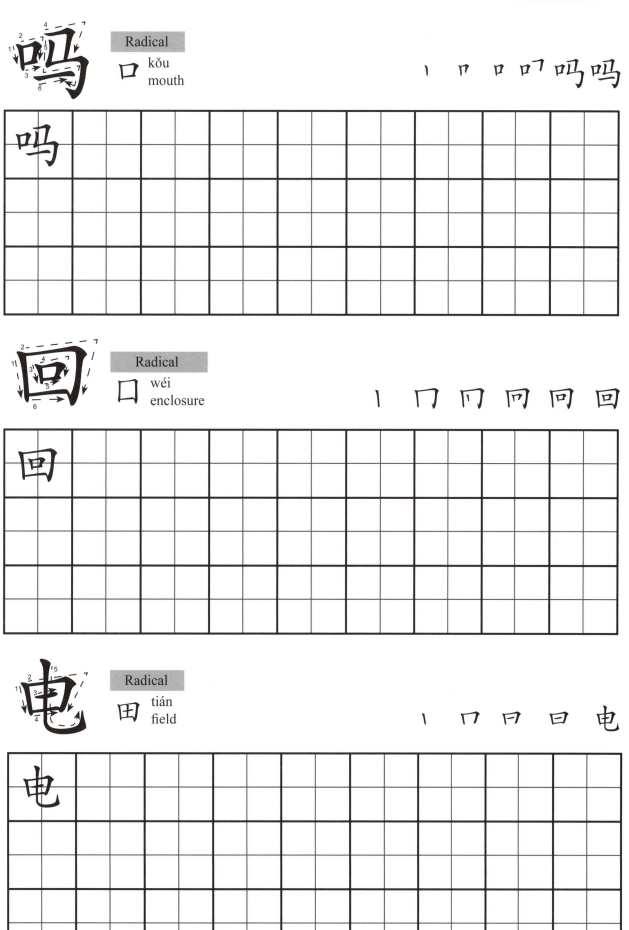

吗

Radical

口 kǒu
mouth

丶 口 口 叫 吗 吗

回

Radical

口 wéi
enclosure

丨 冂 冂 回 回 回

电

Radical

田 tián
field

丨 冂 曰 日 电

 **Radical**
见 jiàn
see

、 ﾗ ﾈ ﾈ 衤 初 初 视 视

视											

Radical
亅 jué
hook

一 ﾗ 戸 戸 写 写 事 事

事											

 **Radical**
扌(手) shǒu
hand

一 扌 扌 扌 找 找 找

找											

到

Radical

刂 (刀) dāo knife

一 乙 云 云 至 至 到 到

课

Radical

讠 (言) yán speech

丶 讠 讠 讥 诏 诏 课 课 课

本

Radical

木 mù wood

一 十 才 木 本

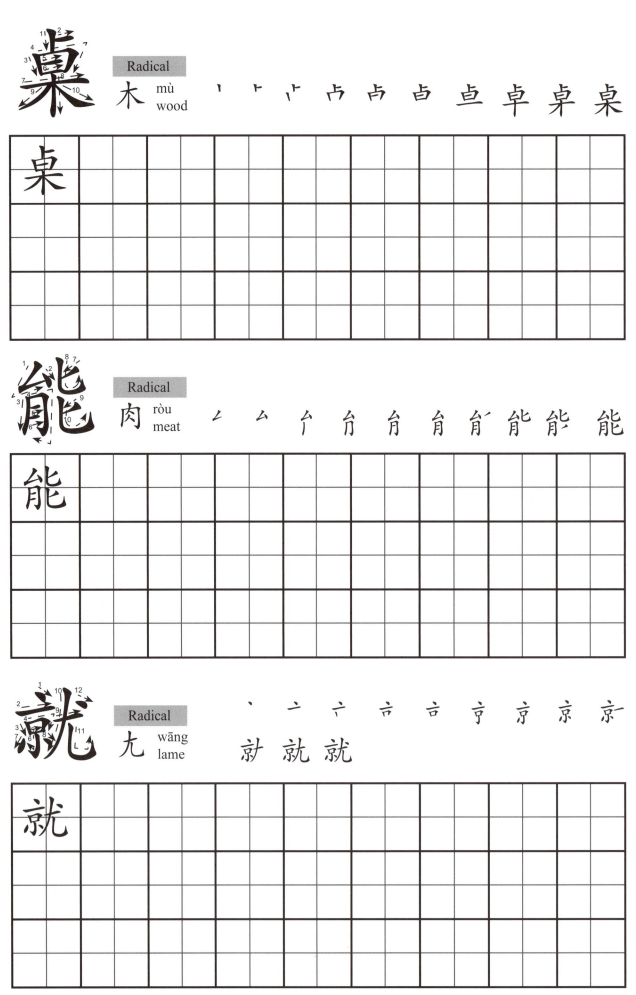

桌

Radical

木 mù wood

丨 丨 卜 卜 占 占 占 卓 卓 桌

桌

能

Radical

肉 ròu meat

ㄥ ㄥ 夂 夂 有 有 育 能 能 能

能

就

Radical

尢 wāng lame

丶 二 六 亠 亠 宁 京 京

尤 就 就

就

沙

Radical

氵(水) shuǐ
water

丶 丶 氵 氵丿 氵丿 氵丿 沙

发

Radical

又 yòu
again

一 丆 丠 发 发

马

Radical

马 mǎ
horse

乛 马 马

I. Choose the picture that best illustrates what you hear.

1. A.   B.   C.   D.

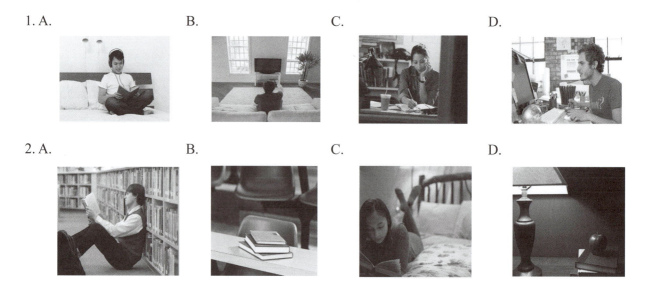

2. A.   B.   C.   D.

II. Listen to the recording and answering the following True or False questions.

(   )   1. Xiaomei makes a phone call to Mali.

(   )   2. Mali is watching TV in the dorm.

(   )   3. Xiaomei cannot find her English textbook.

(   )   4. Xiaomei asks Mali to help look for her English book.

(   )   5. Mali found Xiaomei's book on the sofa.

III. Listen to the recording and answering the following True or False questions.

(   )   1. This telephone conversation is between Dadong and Xiaomei.

(   )   2. Dadong needs Xiaomei's help with his Spanish.

(   )   3. Xiaomei is not willing to help right away because she is watching TV with her roommate.

(   )   4. Xiaomei will meet Dadong at a coffee shop in front of her dorm.

(   )   5. Dadong and Xiaomei will meet each other at 10:30.

I. Xiaomei is looking for her cat. Using the picture below, make an audio recording in which you suggest five possible places the cat may be hiding. Use complete sentences. Use the space below to make note of your ideas, if necessary.

小美：我的小猫会在哪儿呢？

1. 小猫可能在 _____ 。

2. _____ 。

3. _____ 。

4. _____ 。

5. _____ 。

II. A new student from China is going to move into your dorm next week. He wants to know some details about the dorm. Make an audio recording in which you answer his questions. Use the space below to make note of your ideas, if necessary.

1. 宿舍在哪儿？

_____

2. 校园里有健身房吗？

_____

3. 宿舍里面有什么？

_____

4. 校园里有咖啡店吗？

_____

I. Complete the following Structure Note practices.

Structure Note 5.7: Use 在 with an action verb to indicate the location of an activity.

> Subject + 在 + Location + Verb Phrase

A. Rewrite the sentences below by inserting 在 and the appropriate verb.

1. 我 / 教室 / 找我的课本

_____

2. 他们 / 饭馆 / 吃烧鸡

_____

3. 我 / 咖啡店 / 工作

_____

4. 大东和祥安 / 健身房 / 运动

_____

5. 他 / 房间 / 看电视

_____

Structure Note 5.8: Use 到 as a resultative complement to indicate completion of an action.

> Subject + Verb + 到 (+ Object)

B. Write the following sentences in Chinese using 到 as a resultative complement.

1. I saw your dog in your bedroom. _____

2. I made it! _____

3. I will find your book. _____

4. I found the school's library. _____

5. I will go back to Russia. _____

Structure Note 5.9: Use 得 or 不 and a resultative complement to indicate whether it is possible or not possible to reach a result.

Verb + (不 / 得) + Resultative Complement (+ Object)

C. Rearrange the words below and form them into complete sentences.

1. 你 / 法文课本 / 找得到 / 我的 / 吗

   _____

2. 字 / 看不到 / 老师 / 他 / 写的

   _____

3. 看不到 / 室友 / 你的 / 我

   _____

4. 弟弟 / 我 / 找不到 / 的 / 课本

   _____

5. 他的 / 他 / 狗 / 吗 / 找得到

   _____

Structure Note 5.10: Use 可能 to express likelihood.

Subject + 可能 (+ 会) + Verb Phrase

D. Fill in the blanks using 可能, 会 or 可能会.

1. 他 _____ 去健身房。

2. 我明天 _____ 去他的生日派对。

3. 她 _____ 跟大家一起去。

4. 美国人 _____ 不喜欢喝茶。

5. 我的课本 _____ 在哪里呢？

Structure Note 5.11: Use completion 了 to describe completed actions.

$$\boxed{\text{Subject} + \text{Verb (+ Object)} + 了}$$

E. Rewrite the following sentences using 了.

1. 我们昨天看足球比赛。

_____

2. 你吃晚饭吗?

_____

3. 他上午去图书馆。

_____

4. 玛丽喝咖啡。

_____

5. 他们点菜。

_____

Structure Note 5.12: Use 就 to indicate "right" or "precisely."

$$\boxed{\text{Subject} + 就 + \text{Verb (+ Object)}}$$

F. Rewrite the following sentences using 就.

1. 李老师是她的爸爸。

_____

2. 那是我的中文课本。

_____

3. 小猫在我的书桌下。

_____

4. 今天是他的生日。

_____

5. 他在这家咖啡店工作。

I. Read the following passage and answer the questions.

> 安娜是玛丽的新同学。她住在学校外面，在中国餐厅对面和图书馆后面。她没有室友，可是她有一只猫。安娜很喜欢她的猫。她的猫喜欢吃鸡肉。

1. Who is Anna?
   A. She is Mali's student.
   B. She is Mali's friend.
   C. She is Mali's classmate.
   D. She is Mali's roommate.

2. What is NOT true about Anna's living situation?
   A. She lives with a cat.
   B. She lives on campus.
   C. She lives across from a Chinese restaurant.
   D. She has no roomates.

II. Read the following e-mail and answer the questions.

Sender	安娜
Subject	中文课本

同学们：
我找不到我的中文课本，可不可以帮我找一下？书上有我的名字。书可能在咖啡店，也可能在餐厅，还有可能在图书馆。明天就有中文课，请帮我找！谢谢！

1. What is the subject of this e-mail?
   A. Meeting in the library
   B. Hiring in the coffee shop
   C. A missing Chinese book
   D. Chinese class today

2. Which of the following statements is NOT true?
   A. Anna lost her Chinese textbook.
   B. Anna did not put her name on her textbook.
   C. Anna asked her friends to look in three different places.
   D. Anna has her Chinese class tomorrow.

WRITING PRACTICE 5.2

I. Create a dialogue based on the following pictures. Mali calls Anna to ask for help finding her Chinese textbook in her dorm room. Describe a possible location for the book.

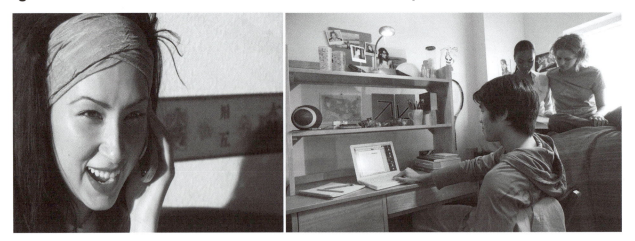

玛丽：安娜，你在哪里？

安娜：_____

玛丽：_____

安娜：_____

玛丽：_____

安娜：_____

II. Write a note to your roommate to tell him or her about a party you will have at a restaurant. Describe the location of the restaurant and what they serve. Include the date and time of the party.

UNIT 6 – LESSON 1

买东西

VOCABULARY REVIEW 6.1

I. Mark the correct tones above the pinyin for the vocabulary below. Read the characters aloud as you mark the tones.

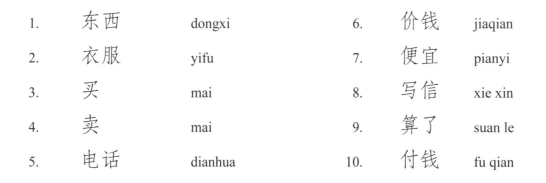

1.	东西	dongxi		6.	价钱	jiaqian
2.	衣服	yifu		7.	便宜	pianyi
3.	买	mai		8.	写信	xie xin
4.	卖	mai		9.	算了	suan le
5.	电话	dianhua		10.	付钱	fu qian

II. Match the vocabulary below with the corresponding pictures.

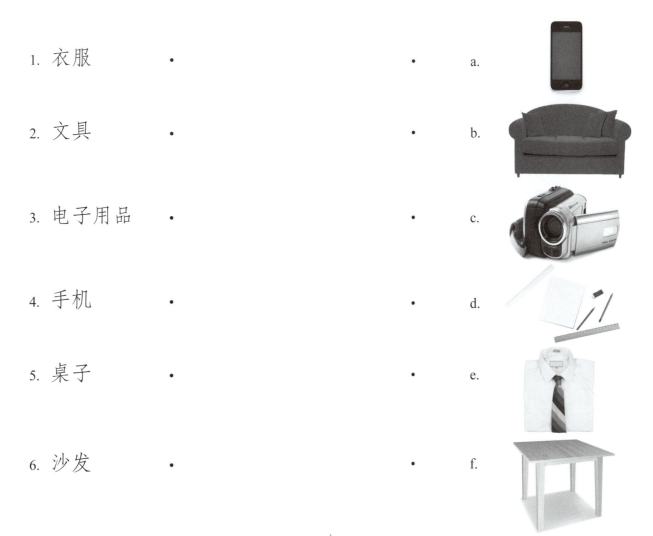

1. 衣服 •

2. 文具 •

3. 电子用品 •

4. 手机 •

5. 桌子 •

6. 沙发 •

      • a.

      • b.

      • c.

      • d.

      • e.

      • f.

Radical

宀 mì
cover

丶 丶 宀 写 写

Radical

乙 yǐ
second
heavenly
stem

一 フ フ 三 买 买

Radical

十 shí
ten

一 十 土 土 丰 丰 卖 卖

Radical

一 yī
one

一 七 坛 东 东

东											

Radical

西 yà
stopper

一 一 冂 丙 西 西

西											

Radical

手 shǒu
hand

一 二 三 手

手											

得　得

Radical
彳 chì step

丿 ノ 彳 彳 彳 彳 彳 彳 彳 得
得 得

得

少

Radical
小 xiǎo small

丨 小 小 少

少

钱

Radical
钅(金) jīn gold

丿 𠂊 𠂉 钅 钅 钅 钅 钱
钱 钱

钱

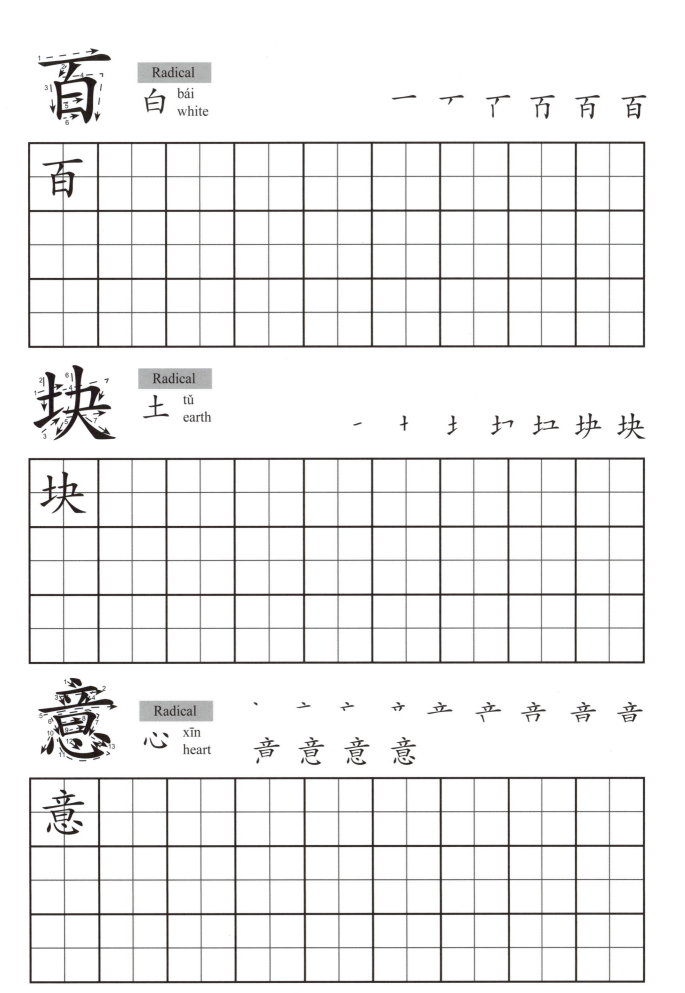

一 ブ ア 万 百 百

Radical
白 bái
white

Radical
土 tǔ
earth

一 十 土 圠 圠 块 块

Radical
心 xīn
heart

、 二 六 亠 立 产 音 音 音
音 意 意 意

思 **Radical** 心 xīn heart 丶 口 口 田 田 **甲** 思 思 思

价 **Radical** 亻(人) rén person 丿 亻 亻 价 价 价

信 **Radical** 亻(人) rén person 丿 亻 亻 仁 佇 信 信 信 信

I. Listen to the recording and answer the following True or False questions.

( ) 1. The store sells cell phones, stationery, and televisions.

( ) 2. The woman wants to buy a computer.

( ) 3. The woman doesn't like to buy cheap items.

( ) 4. The man recommends a cell phone that costs $199.

( ) 5. The woman finally buys the cell phone in the store.

II. Listen to the recording and answer the following True or False questions.

( ) 1. The woman is going shopping for herself.

( ) 2. The man wants to go shopping with the woman.

( ) 3. The woman wants to buy a book for Zhongping.

( ) 4. The book costs $25.

( ) 5. The woman buys the book.

III. Listen to the recording and answer the following True or False questions.

( ) 1. The price of the first cell phone was $500.

( ) 2. The man is trying to sell the cell phone to the woman.

( ) 3. Bargaining is not permitted at the store.

( ) 4. The woman shows another more expensive phone to the man.

( ) 5. The man buys the phone that costs $350.99.

SPEAKING PRACTICE 6.1

I. Make an audio recording in which you are in a department store and ask the price of an item. You try to bargain with the clerk but in the end decide not to buy the item. Use the space below to make note of your ideas, if necessary.

A: _____?

B: 这_____要四百四十九块九毛九。

A: _____?

B: 不好意思，我们这里不讲价。

A: _____。

II. Look at the pictures below. Roleplay a customer asking the clerk for the price of each item. Answer accordingly.

$90

$65

$799.99

$8.25

$176.50

$150.95

STRUCTURE REVIEW 6.1

I. Complete the following Structure Note practices.

Structure Note 6.1: Use 有 to express existence rather than possession.

> (Location +) 有 + Noun Phrase

A. Write the following sentences in Chinese using 有 to express existence.

1. The school has Chinese students. _____

2. Are there Chinese books in the library? _____

3. There is a gym in the school. _____

4. This restaurant doesn't have chopsticks. _____

5. That shop has stationery. _____

Structure Note 6.2: Use 得 to express "must."

> Subject + 得 + Verb Phrase

B. Substitute 要 with 得 in the following sentences to indicate "must."

1. 玛丽今天要见王老师。_____

2. 我明天要去工作。_____

3. 你要给你爸爸妈妈写信。_____

4. 他要去图书馆看书。_____

5. 我要找我的手机。_____

Structure Note 6.3: Use 给 as the preposition "to."

> Subject + 给 + Object + Verb Phrase

C. Use the given words and the pattern above to form complete sentences.

1. 朋友 / 打电话 _____

2. 老师 / 写信 _____

3. 弟弟 / 打电话 _____

4. 爸爸妈妈 / 写信 _____

5. 室友 / 打电话 _____

Structure Note 6.4: Use 多少 to ask "how many" or "how much."

> Subject (+ Verb) + 多少 + Noun

D. Write the following sentences in Chinese using 多少 / 几.

1. How much is this cell phone? _____

2. How many Chinese books do you have? _____

3. How many roommates do you have? _____

4. How much is your cell phone? _____

5. How many family members do you have? _____

Structure Note 6.5: Use Adjectives with （一）点（儿）to express "a little more."

> Subject + Adjective + （一）点（儿）

E. Write the following sentences in Chinese using （一）点（儿）.

1. This cell phone is a little more expensive. _____

2. This Hot and Sour soup is a little more spicy. _____

3. This restaurant is a little nicer. _____

4. I want one a little cheaper. _____

5. His room is little bigger. _____

Structure Note 6.6: Use 还是……吧 to express a suggested alternative.

> Subject + 还是 + Verb Phrase + 吧

F. Read the scenarios below. Choose the correct alternative from the options provided using 还是……吧.

1. 我不喜欢吃北京烤鸭。(吃中国菜 / 吃法国菜)

   _____

2. 安娜很想爸爸妈妈，可是没有手机。(写信 / 打电话)

   _____

3. 中平不喜欢看足球比赛。(去看足球比赛 / 去图书馆看书)

   _____

4. 后天是玛丽的生日，她想要新的手机。(给她买礼物 / 请她吃饭)

   _____

5. 他很想吃饺子，可是这家饭馆不卖饺子。(吃米饭 / 喝茶)

   _____

READING COMPREHENSION 6.1

I. Read the following passage and answer the questions.

> 后天是安娜爸爸的生日。安娜要给她爸爸买礼物。安娜想买手机。安娜的爸爸喜欢的手机是三百九十九块。太贵了！安娜不想买手机了。算了，还是给爸爸买衣服吧！

1. Which of the following statement is correct?
   A. It is Anna's birthday tomorrow.
   B. It is Anna's father's birthday tomorrow.
   C. It is Anna's father's birthday the day after tomorrow.
   D. It was Anna's father's birthday yesterday.

2. How much did the cell phone cost?
   A. $300.00　　B. $400.00
   C. $399.00　　D. $299.00

3. What did Anna decide to buy?
   A. She will buy the phone.
   B. She will buy a computer.
   C. She will not buy anything.
   D. She will buy her dad some clothes.

II. Read the following passage and answer the questions.

> 秀水街 (Xiù Shuǐ Jiē, Silk Alley) 是一个很大的商店。秀水街卖很多东西，有衣服、文具，还有电子用品。中国人喜欢去秀水街买便宜的东西，在那儿可以讲价。每天都会有很多人去那里买东西。在秀水街可以买中国的用品 (ex:中国衣服和桌子)，可以吃北京烤鸭，也可以喝咖啡！秀水街在故宫 (Gùgōng, Palace Museum) 的东边、天坛 (Tiāntán, Temple of Heaven) 的北边。

1. Where is Silk Alley located in Beijing?
   A. North of the Palace Musuem, South of the Temple of Heaven.
   B. East of the Palace Museum, South of the Temple of Heaven.
   C. East of the Palace Museum, North of the Temple of Heaven.
   D. West of the Palace Museum, North of the Temple of Heaven.

2. What items are sold at the Silk Alley that were mentioned in the passage?
   A. Clothes
   B. Electronics
   C. Tables
   D. All of the above

3. What else can you do at the Silk Alley that was mentioned in the passage?
   A. Watch a sports game
   B. Buy movie tickets
   C. Eat Peking Duck
   D. All of the above

WRITING PRACTICE 6.1

I. Write about a recent shopping trip. Where did you go? What did you buy? Who did you buy the item for? How much did it cost? Record the details in Chinese in the table below.

Store	Item	Quantity	Price	For whom?

Total: _____

II. Based on the information in the table, write a paragraph about your shopping trip.

VOCABULARY REVIEW 6.2

I. Mark the correct tones above the pinyin for the vocabulary below. Read the characters aloud as you mark the tones.

1.	已经	yijing	8.	项链	xianglian
2.	功课	gongke	9.	现金	xianjin
3.	所以	suoyi	10.	刷卡	shua ka
4.	不用	bu yong	11.	收	shou
5.	再	zai	12.	问题	wenti
6.	这么	zheme	13.	付	fu
7.	条	tiao	14.	别的	bie de

II. Match the vocabulary below with the corresponding pictures.

1. 钱包 •

        • a.

2. 商店 •

        • b.

3. 现金 •

        • c.

        • d.

4. 项链 •

5. 信用卡 •

        • e.

CHARACTER WRITING PRACTICE 6.2

问

Radical
门 mén
door

、　丨　门　门　问　问

问									

再

Radical
冂 jiōng
down box

一　厂　万　丙　再　再

再									

现

Radical
王 wáng
king

一　二　干　王　玑　玑　现　现

现									

 **Radical**

人 rén
person

ﾚ ﾚ ﾚ 以 以

以											

话 **Radical**

讠(言) yán
speech

丶 讠 讠 讠 讵 话 话 话

话											

 **Radical**

己 jǐ
self

一 コ 已

已											

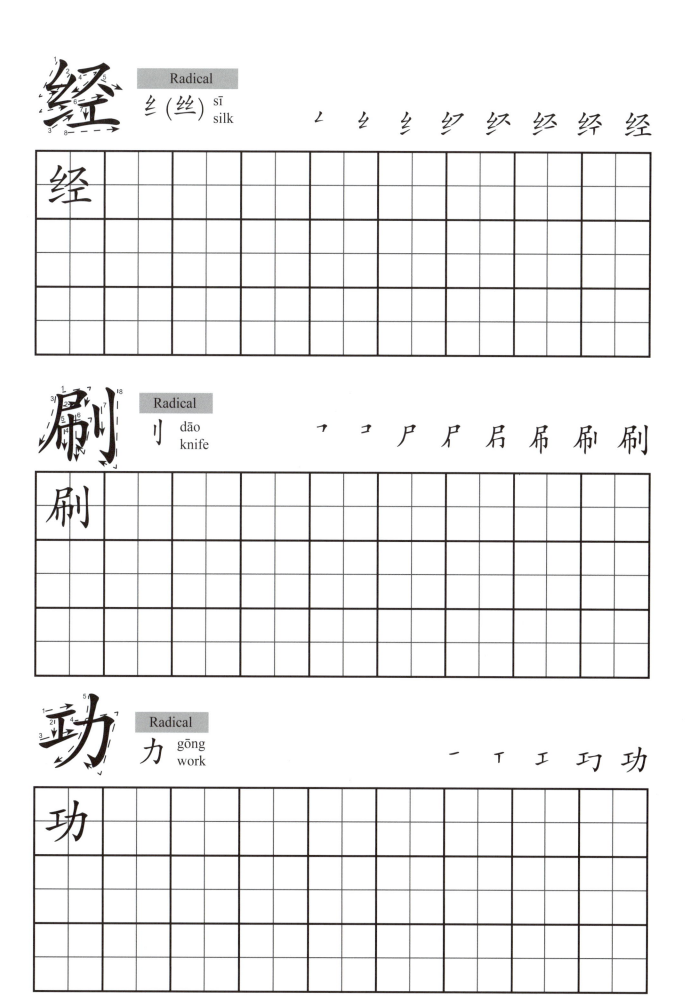

経

丝 (糸) sī silk **Radical**

刷

刂 dāo knife **Radical**

动

力 gōng work **Radical**

Radical

户 hù
door

丶 广 户 户 戸 所 所 所

所								

Radical

金 jīn
gold

丿 人 人 今 全 全 金 金

金								

收

Radical

攵(攴) pū
knock

𡿨 丩 收 收 收 收

收								

花

Radical
艹(草) cǎo grass

一 十 艹 艹 艹 花 花

花											

题

Radical
页 yè page

丨 冂 日 日 旦 早 早 杲 是
是 起 起 题 题 题

题											

行

Radical
彳 chì step

丿 彳 彳 彳 行 行

行											

I. Listen to the recording and answer the questions.

1. Where is Zhongping going?
   A. library   B. office   C. shop   D. cafeteria

2. What is Zhongping going to do?
   A. grocery shopping   B. eat dinner   C. buy a gift for Mali

3. What is Zhongping planning to buy?
   A. a cake   B. a necklace   C. a cell phone   D. a computer

4. What does Zhongping's friend say about his plan?
   A. A necklace is too expensive as a present.
   B. A necklace is an ideal gift.
   C. There's no need to give Mali another birthday present.
   D. Mali will like the present.

5. How old will Mali be tomorrow?
   A. 12   B. 20   C. 21   D. 22

II. Listen to the recording and answer the following True or False questions.

( ) 1. This telephone conversation is between Dadong and Anna.

( ) 2. Dadong needs Xiaomei's help with buying something.

( ) 3. They will meet tomorrow at 1PM.

( ) 4. Dadong is buying a birthday gift for his mother.

( ) 5. Xiaomei agrees to help Dadong.

III. Listen to the recording and answer the questions.

1. How much is the necklace?
   A. $502   B. $509   C. $529   D. $592

2. How does the man pay for the necklace?
   A. credit card   B. cash   C. check

3. Which statement is NOT true?
   A. The man tries to bargain for a cheaper price.
   B. The store does not allow bargaining.
   C. The man gives the clerk $550.
   D. The change the man gets is $71.

SPEAKING PRACTICE 6.2

I. Make an audio recording in which you answer the following questions based on the lesson text from Unit 6 Lesson 2.

1. 李中平为什么要买礼物送给玛丽？

   _____ 。

2. 李中平想买什么给玛丽？

   _____ 。

3. 陈大东对李中平说什么？

   _____ 。

4. 如果礼物太贵的话，李中平怎么办？

   _____ 。

5. 要是你是李中平，你会买那么贵的礼物吗？为什么？

   _____ 。

II. Make an audio recording in which you are buying a necklace for your friend at a department store. Tell the sales clerk that you would like to buy the necklace, and tell him that you will pay for it in cash.

A: _____ 。

B: 好，这条项链的价钱是五十五块。 请问，您是付现金还是刷卡？

A: _____ 。

B: 收您六十块，找您五块。谢谢！

A: _____ 。

I. Complete the following Structure Note practices.

Structure Note 6.7: Use 再 to indicate a repeating action.

> Subject + 再 + Verb Phrase

A. Write the following sentences in Chinese using 再.

1. I want to buy another present for her.

_____

2. Let's go to the store again tomorrow.

_____

3. He will call his parents again on the phone next week.

_____

4. (Create your own sentence)

_____

5. (Create your own sentence)

_____

Structure Note 6.8: Use 因为···所以··· to express causal relationships.

> (因为 +) Phrase, + (所以 +) Phrase

B. Fill in the blanks in the sentences using the 因为···所以··· sentence pattern.

1. _____今天是你生日，_____我请客。

2. _____他帮我找课本，_____我要谢谢他。

3. _____妈妈不在家，_____爸爸做晚饭。

4. (Create your own sentence)

_____

5. (Create your own sentence)

_____

Structure Note 6.9: Use 不用 to say "need not."

> Subject + 不用 + Verb Phrase

C. Rewrite the following sentences using 不用.

1. 我得买这本书。 _____

2. 他得马上给小美打电话。 _____

3. 你得送玛丽很贵的礼物。 _____

4. 我得去商店买衣服。 _____

5. 他星期六得在咖啡店工作。 _____

Strucutre Note 6.10: Use 这么 or 那么 to intensify adjectives.

> 这么 / 那么 + Adjective

D. Rewrite the sentences below by adding 这么 or 那么 to an appropriate place.

1. 谢谢你送我好吃的蛋糕。

_____

2. 你写的汉字很好看。

_____

3. 你的学校很大！

_____

4. 我不想要很贵的礼物。

_____

5. 我不喜欢吃很辣的菜。

_____

Strucutre Note 6.11: Use verb + 了 to describe specific completed actions.

> Subject + Verb + 了 (+ Quantity) + Object

E. Write the following sentences in Chinese using "verb + 了".

1. She drank so much coffee.

_____

2. Yesterday I bought two books.

_____

3. I drank two cups of tea this morning.

_____

4. (Create your own sentence)

_____

5. (Create your own sentence)

_____

Structure Note 6.12: Use 已经 to express "already."

> Subject + 已经 + Verb Phrase (+ 了)

F. Write the following sentences in Chinese using 已经……了.

1. She has already bought a cell phone.

_____

2. They have already eaten three plates of dumplings.

_____

3. He has already gone to Japan.

_____

4. (Create your own sentence)

_____

5. (Create your own sentence)

_____

Strucutre Note 6.13: Use 要是···（的话）···就··· to say "if . . ., then . . ."

要是 + Sentence (+ 的话), Subject + 就 + Verb Phrase

G. Fill in the blanks using the "要是···（的话）···就···" sentence pattern.

1. _____ 你昨天来玛丽的生日派对，_____ 会见到我了。
2. _____ 他明天去文具店，我 _____ 跟他一起去。
3. _____ 你没有现金 _____，_____ 刷卡吧！

4. (Create your own sentence)

_____

5. (Create your own sentence)

_____

Strucutre Note 6.14: Use （是）···还是··· to express either-or questions.

Subject (+ 是) + Verb Phrase / Noun + 还是 + Verb Phrase / Noun

H. Create sentences using the "是···还是···" pattern and the given words.

1. 我们 / 先吃饭 / 先做作业

_____

2. 你 / 喜欢中国菜 / 法国菜

_____

3. 你哥哥 / 学法语 / 西班牙语

_____

4. 他们 / 住在宿舍 / 住在家里

_____

5. 课本 / 放在卧室里 / 客厅里

_____

I. Read the following dialogue and answer the questions in Chinese.

中平说想买一份生日礼物送给玛丽，他的朋友大东问他想买什么，中平说想买一条项链给玛丽。

大东：你不用买这么贵的礼物啊！要是你买项链的话，你就没有钱买别的东西了！

中平：我很想买！

大东：你是不是喜欢玛丽啊？

中平：没错！我很喜欢玛丽，所以我想送她一份很好的礼物。

1. Why does Zhongping want to buy a present for Mali?

_____

2. What does Zhongping plan to buy for Mali?

_____

3. Does Dadong like his idea? Why or why not?

_____

4. What is the real reason that Zhongping wants to buy such an expensive present for Mali?

_____

II. Read the following passage and answer the questions.

上星期六，我请几个朋友去饭馆吃午饭，我们点了两盘饺子、一份青菜、一只烧鸡，还有一碗酸辣汤。吃完饭后，我去付钱， 一共是四十八块五毛。我要刷卡，可是服务员说他们只收现金。

我跟我的朋友说："不好意思！因为这家饭馆不刷卡，所以今天我不能请客了！"我的朋友说："没关系！今天还是我请客吧。"服务员说："收您一百块，找您五十一块五毛！"

1. Which of the following statements is correct?
   A. They ordered two bowls of Hot and Sour Soup.
   B. They ordered three orders of roast chicken.
   C. They ordered two plates of dumplings.
   D. They ordered one plate of dumplings.

2. Which statement is NOT true?
   A. The narrator went out for lunch with his friends last Saturday.
   B. The narrator and his friends went to a Spanish restaurant.
   C. The restaurant accepted cash only.
   D. The meal cost $48.50.

3. Why didn't the narrator treat his friends?
   A. He forgot to bring his wallet.
   B. He didn't want to treat his friends.
   C. He forgot to bring his credit card.
   D. He had no cash.

4. How much change did they receive?
   A. $5.50
   B. $55.00
   C. $50.00
   D. $51.50

WRITING PRACTICE 6.2

I. Narrate a complete story as suggested by the pictures. Give your story a beginning, middle, and an end.

(lined writing space)

II. Write a diary entry about shopping using the words provided below.

付	收	找	现金	刷卡	没问题	已经	花

(lined writing space)

UNIT 7 — LESSON 1

放假的计划

VOCABULARY REVIEW 7.1

I. Mark the correct tones above the pinyin for the vocabulary below. Read the characters aloud as you mark the tones.

1.	放假	fang jia	11.	飞机票	feiji piao
2.	计划	jihua	12.	火车票	huoche piao
3.	打算	dasuan	13.	寒假	hanjia
4.	出生	chusheng	14.	但是	danshi
5.	长大	zhangda	15.	北京	Beijing
6.	的时候	de shihou	16.	加州	Jiazhou
7.	好玩儿	haowanr	17.	老家	laojia
8.	烤鸭	kaoya	18.	长城	Changcheng
9.	地方	difang	19.	故宫	Gugong
10.	回家	hui jia			

II. Fill in the blanks for the following vocabulary.

1. to go on vacation _____假

   winter vacation _____假

2. to go home _____家

   hometown _____家

3. birthday 生_____

   to be born _____生

4. travel _____行

   bank _____行

5. bus ticket _____票

   plane ticket _____票

6. thing 东_____

   east, south, west, north 东_____

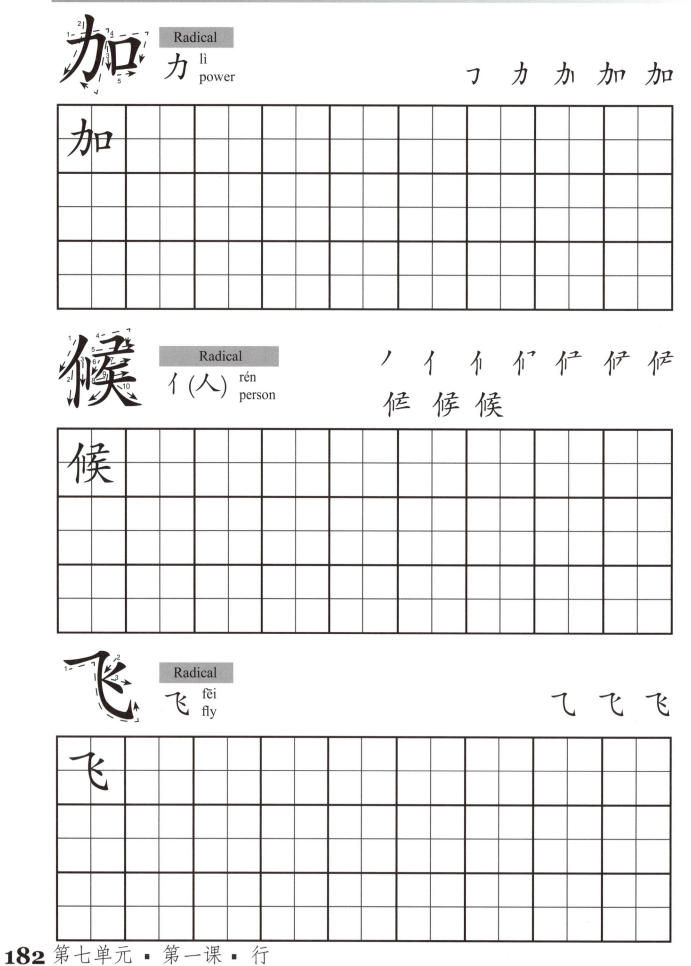

加 Radical
力 lì power

フ 力 加 加 加

加

候 Radical
亻(人) rén person

ノ イ 亻 仃 仃 伊 伊
伊 侯 候

候

飞 Radical
飞 fēi fly

て 飞 飞

飞

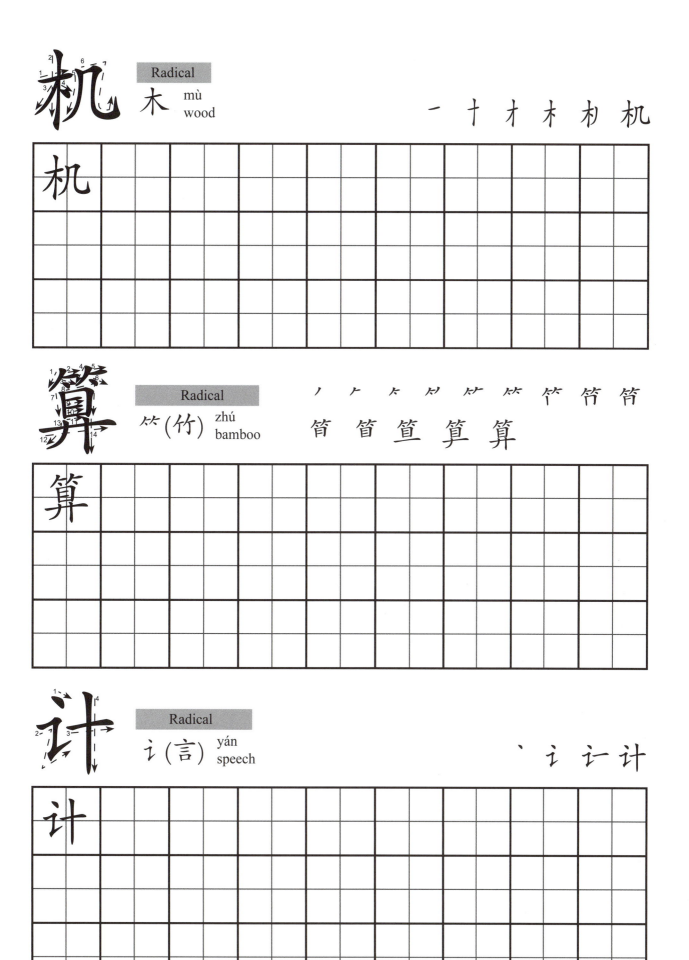

机 木 mù wood   Radical

一 十 才 木 朳 机

算 ⺮(竹) zhú bamboo   Radical

丿 ⺮ ⺮ ⺮ 竹 竹 竹 竿 笃
笥 筲 算 算 算

计 讠(言) yán speech   Radical

丶 讠 计 计

Radical

匕 bǐ
ladle

丨 ㅏ ㅓ ㅓ 北

北

Radical

亠 tóu
lid

丶 亠 宀 市 古 宁 亨 京

京

Radical

人 rén
person

丿 人 从 从

从

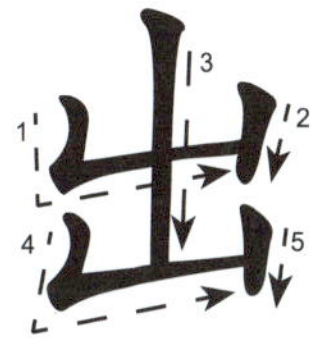

出

Radical
凵 kǎn
open box

ㄴ ㄴ ㅕ 出 出

长

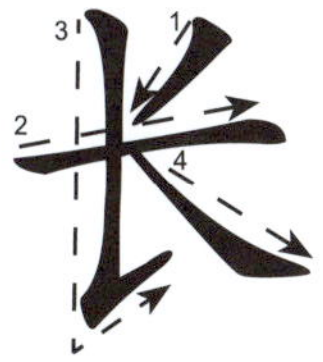

Radical
长 cháng/zhǎng
long/grow

ノ ㅑ 长 长

地

Radical
土 tǔ
earth

一 十 土 圤 地 地

| Radical | 爫 (爪) | zhǎo
claw |

一　一　ㄏ　㲋　㲋　㲋　㲋

旁　爱

爱									

| Radical | 车 | chē
cart |

一　七　左　车

车									

| Radical | 方 | fāng
square |

、　一　亍　方

方									

I. Listen to the recording and answer the following True or False questions.

(   )   1. The man will go to Beijing for summer vacation.

(   )   2. The man plans to leave this Saturday.

(   )   3. The man will take a vacation for 2 months.

(   )   4. The man and the woman will see each other in February.

(   )   5. The woman will go to see her family in Boston.

II. Listen to the recording and answer the following True or False questions.

(   )   1. The woman was born in Boston.

(   )   2. The man grew up in China.

(   )   3. The man came to America when he was 12.

(   )   4. The woman wants to travel to Beijing.

(   )   5. The man invites the woman to go to Beijing with him.

III. Listen to the recording and answer the following True or False questions.

(   )   1. The students are about to have their winter vacation.

(   )   2. Xiang'an will go back to South Africa to visit his family.

(   )   3. Zhongping will go to Spain with his parents.

(   )   4. Mali plans to go to Boston to see her family.

(   )   5. The bus ticket is too expensive, so Mali will stay at the dorm.

I. Listen to the audio recording. Say an appropriate response to each sentence you hear. Use the space below to make note of your ideas, if necessary.

1. Your Response: _____

2. Your Response: _____

3. Your Response: _____

4. Your Response: _____

5. Your Response: _____

II. Make an audio recording in which you discuss your plans for the vacation. In the recording, include the places you will go, how you will get there, who you will go with, the dates you will leave and return, and how much it will cost. Use the space below to make note of your ideas, if necessary.

I. Complete the following Structure Note practices.

Structure Note 7.1: Use 的时候 to create "when" expressions.

> Subject + Verb Phrase or Time Expression + 的时候 + Verb Phrase

A. Using the given prompts, write complete sentences in Chinese with 的时候.

1. vacation / plan? _____

2. watch TV / drink tea_____

3. three years old / come to USA _____

4. in Beijing / eat Beijing duck _____

5. birthday / eat cake _____

Structure Note 7.2: Use 才 to indicate an action occurring later than anticipated.

> Subject + Time Expression + 才 + Verb Phrase

B. Make complete sentences in Chinese with the given prompts and the sentence pattern above.

1. 11:30 p.m. / come home _____

2. 10 a.m. / eat breakfast _____

3. next week / soccer game _____

4. last night / do homework _____

5. 20 years old / start to learn English _____

Structure Note 7.3: Use 从 with a place word to indicate origin.

> Subject + 从 + Location + Verb Phrase

C. Make complete sentences in Chinese with the given prompts and the sentence pattern above.

1. Beijing / come to Boston _____

2. dorm / go to cafeteria _____

3. California / call her parents _____

4. (Create your own sentence) _____

5. (Create your own sentence) _____

Structure Note 7.4: Use 是……的 to emphasize the time, locale, or manner of a completed action.

> Subject + 是 + Location / Time / Manner Expression + Verb + Object + 的

> Subject + 是 + Location / Time / Manner Expression + Verb + 的 + Object

D. Use the 是……的 pattern and the given words to form complete sentences.

1. 他 / 从加州 / 来 _____

2. 烤鸭 / 在饭馆 / 买 _____

3. 你 / 在哪里 / 长大 / ? _____

4. 课本 / 在沙发下 / 找到 _____

5. 我 / 1991 年 / 出生 _____

READING COMPREHENSION 7.1

I. Read the following passage and answer the questions.

王小美是玛丽的同屋，她今年二十岁，她的老家在北京。放寒假的时候，她打算回北京看她的爸妈和朋友。玛丽会说一点儿汉语。要是明年可以去北京的话，玛丽想去故宫和长城，还要去吃北京烤鸭。

1. What statement is NOT true?
   A. Xiaomei and Mali are roommates.
   B. Xiaomei is 20 years old.
   C. Beijing is Xiaomei's hometown.
   D. Mali is visiting Beijing this summer.

2. Why is Xiaomei going to Beijing?
   A. Someone recommended she go visit the city.
   B. She has never been to China.
   C. She will visit her parents and friends.
   D. She can practice speaking Chinese.

3. What statement is NOT true about Mali's vacation plans?
   A. Mali will go to Beijing next year.
   B. Mali will visit the Great Wall and the Forbidden City.
   C. Mali will go eat Beijing Duck.
   D. Mali will visit Xiaomei's family.

II. Read the following passage and answer the questions.

因为大东学西班牙文，他暑假很想去西班牙，可是暑假的飞机票都很贵。去西班牙的机票要一千八百块，大东只有七百块钱，所以他今年寒假不能去。要是明年飞机票便宜一点儿的话，他可能会去。

1. Why does Dadong want to travel to Spain ?
   A. Because he comes from Spain.
   B. Because he studies Spanish.
   C. Because the flight tickets are cheap.
   D. Because he will visit his parents there.

2. What statement is NOT true?
   A. Dadong is planning to go to Spain.
   B. Dadong has $1800.
   C. Dadong is $1100 short of buying the flight tickets to Spain.
   D. Dadong might go to Spain next year if the price of flight tickets goes down.

WRITING PRACTICE 7.1

I. Fill in the blanks on the travel log below. What scenic spots and famous dishes were there in Beijing? How long was the trip? How much did the trip cost?

II. Email Response: Read the following email and, based on the information you have recorded above, write or type your response.

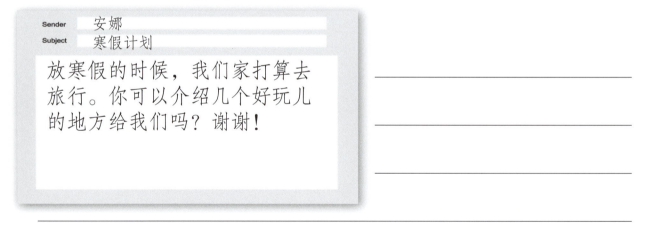

Sender	安娜
Subject	寒假计划

放寒假的时候，我们家打算去旅行。你可以介绍几个好玩儿的地方给我们吗？谢谢！

UNIT 7 – LESSON 2

VOCABULARY REVIEW 7.2

I. Mark the correct tones above the pinyin for the vocabulary below. Read the characters aloud as you mark the tones.

1.	飞机场	feijichang	9.	往左转	wang zuo zhuan
2.	怎么走	zenme zou	10.	别吵	bie chao
3.	开车	kai che	11.	知道	zhidao
4.	路口	lukou	12.	穿过	chuan guo
5.	应该	yinggai	13.	离	li
6.	迷路	mi lu	14.	然后	ranhou
7.	小心	xiaoxin	15.	不用谢	bu yong xie
8.	大街	dajie	16.	一直	yizhi

II. Write the following words in Chinese characters.

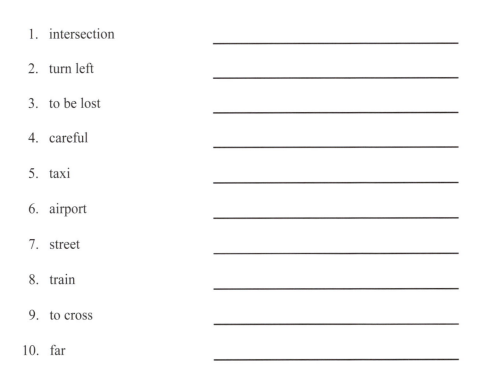

1. intersection _____

2. turn left _____

3. to be lost _____

4. careful _____

5. taxi _____

6. airport _____

7. street _____

8. train _____

9. to cross _____

10. far _____

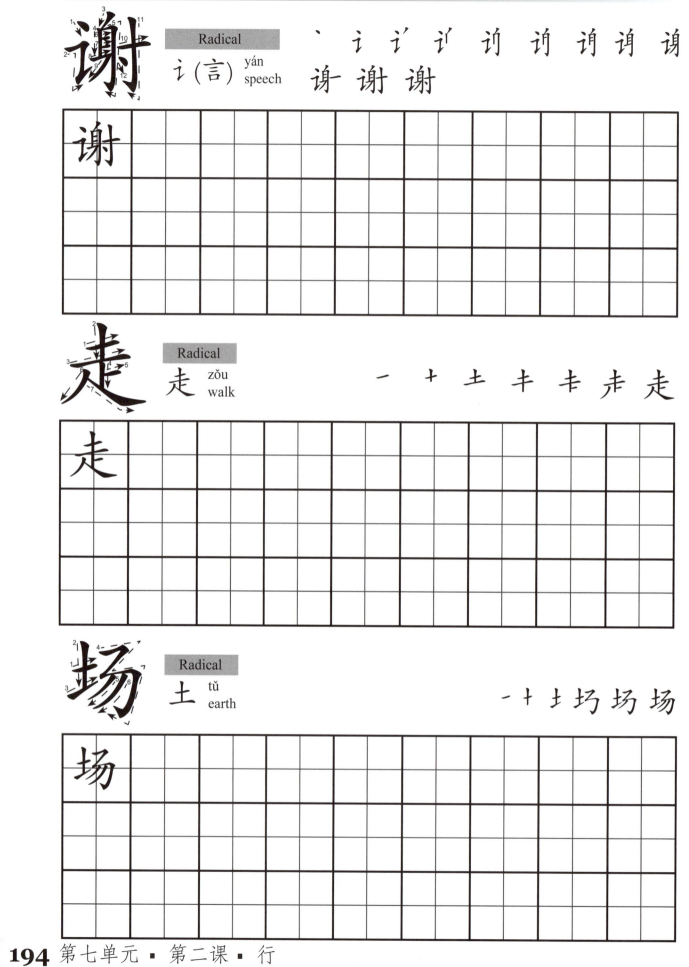

谢

Radical

讠(言) yán speech

丶 讠 讠 讠 讱 讱 讱 讱 讱
讱 谢 谢

谢

走

Radical

走 zǒu walk

一 十 土 卡 走 走 走

走

场

Radical

土 tǔ earth

一 十 土 圢 场 场

场

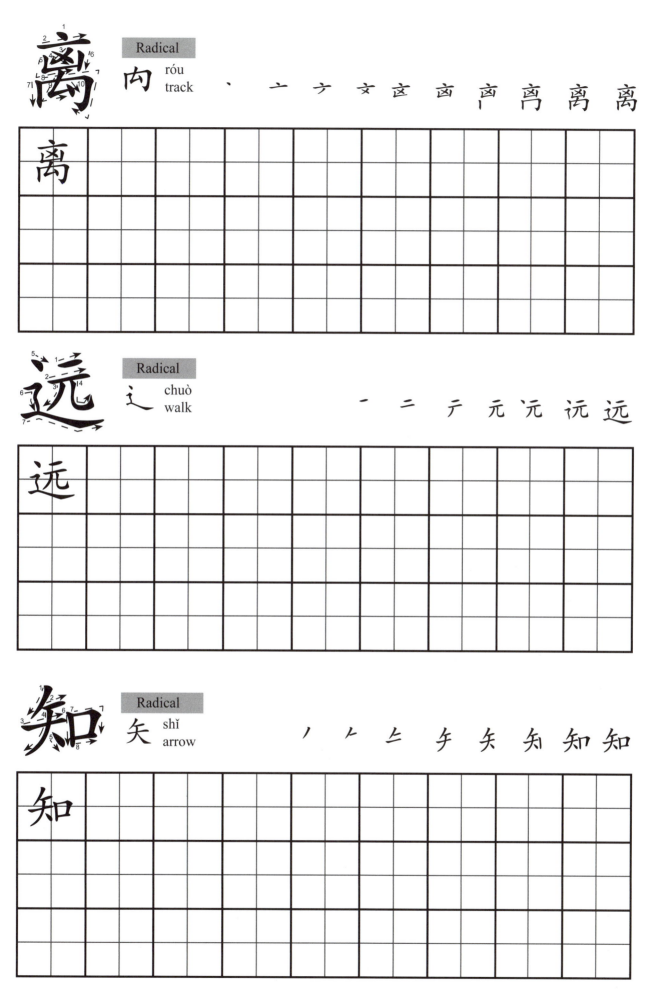

離　Radical

內 róu
track

、　一　ナ　文　攵　卤　卤　离　离　离

离

遠　Radical

辶 chuò
walk

一　二　干　元　元　远　远

远

知　Radical

矢 shǐ
arrow

丿　㇒　㇠　午　矢　知　知　知

知

Radical

彳 chì
step

ノ ク イ イ 行 行 往 往

往										

Radical

工 gōng
work

一 ナ た た 左

左										

Radical

口 kǒu
mouth

一 ナ オ 右 右

右										

转

Radical
车 chē
cart

一 ナ 午 车 车 车 车 转 转

应

Radical
广 guǎng
shelter

丶 亠 广 广 广 应 应

该

Radical
讠(言) yán
speech

丶 讠 讠 讠 讠 该 该 该

Radical

口 kǒu
mouth

一 厂 厂 斤 后 后

后

Radical

小 xiǎo
small

亅 小 小

小

Radical

心 xīn
heart

丶 心 心 心

心

I. Listen to the recording and answer the following questions.

1. Where was Zhongping originally going?
   - A. library
   - B. Mali's place
   - C. department store
   - D. cafeteria

2. What is Anna asking Zhongping for?
   - A. a ride to the library
   - B. a ride to Mali's dorm
   - C. a ride to the airport
   - D. a ride to the department store

3. Which statement is NOT true?
   - A. Mali's house is not far from the library.
   - B. Zhongping doesn't know how to get to Mali's house.
   - C. Anna is going to Mali's house.
   - D. Zhongping gave Mali a ride home yesterday.

II. Listen to the conversation and answer the following questions.

1. Where do you think the conversation occurred ?
   - A. in a car
   - B. at a bus stop
   - C. at the train station
   - D. at the airport

2. What are they going to do?
   - A. travel to America
   - B. travel to China
   - C. pick up Xiaomei
   - D. pick up their American friend

3. What statement is NOT true?
   - A. The airport is not far from the man's house.
   - B. Xiaomei has been in America for two years.
   - C. Xiaomei's roommate is French.
   - D. Xiaomei's roommate will come to Beijing with her.

4. What is the correct way to get to the airport?
   - A. Turn right at the intersection.
   - B. Cross the street first and then turn right.
   - C. Turn left at the intersection.
   - D. Turn right first and then cross the street.

III. Listen to the conversation and answer the following questions.

1. What was Xiaomei's plan for the winter break?
   - A. Travel to Europe
   - B. Go back to her hometown
   - C. Drive to Boston
   - D. Stay at campus

2. How long will it take to drive to Boston?
   - A. about 2 hours
   - B. about 10 hours
   - C. about 12 hours
   - D. about 20 hours

3. What statement is NOT true?
   - A. Xiaomei's hometown is Beijing.
   - B. The man invites Xiaomei to go to Boston with him.
   - C. The man will drive to Boston.
   - D. Xiaomei thinks the flight ticket to Boston is very cheap.

I. You meet a tourist who asks you for directions. Make an audio recording in which you answer his/her questions according to the map below.

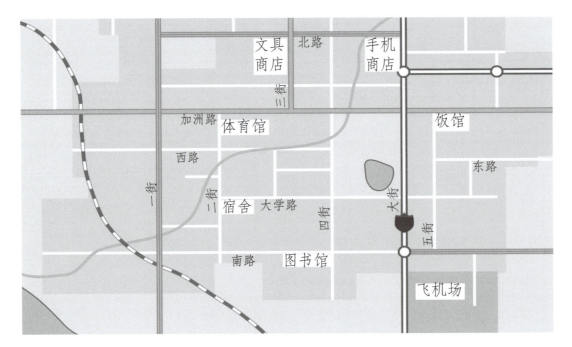

1. 请问从飞机场到宿舍怎么走？

2. 请问从宿舍到图书馆怎么走？

3. 请问从体育馆到饭馆怎么走？

4. 请问从手机商店到文具商店怎么走？

5. 请问从文具商店到图书馆怎么走？

II. Using the map above, make an audio recording in which you take a taxi to the library and need to give the driver directions. You may choose any location on the map as your starting point.

A: 你要去哪里？

B: _____。

A: 到图书馆怎么走？

B: _____

_____。

STRUCTURE REVIEW 7.2

I. Complete the following Structure Note practices.

Structure Note 7.5: Use 送······去 to mean "take."

| Subject (+ Means of Transport) + 送 + Object + 去 / 到 + Location |

A. Write the following sentences in Chinese using the 送······去 pattern.

1. Dad drives my younger sister to the library.

_____

2. Could you take us to the airport?

_____

3. Please give her a ride to the dorm.

_____

4. Who drove you back home last night?

_____

5. I need to drive my friend to the bookstore tomorrow morning.

_____

Structure Note 7.6: Use 离 to express location relative to a reference point.

| Location A + 离 + Location B + Adjective Distance Phrase |

B. Use the vocabulary below to make five sentences with the given sentence structure.

| 飞机场　图书馆　饭馆　商店　学校 |
| 宿舍　文具商店　近　远 |

1. _____

2. _____

3. _____

4. _____

5. _____

Structure Note 7.7: Use 到 with place words to indicate destination.

> Subject (+ 从 + Location A) (+ 到 + Location B) + Verb Phrase

C. Use the vocabulary below to make five sentences with the given sentence structure.

> 飞机场　图书馆　饭馆　商店　学校
> 宿舍　文具商店　近　远

1. _____

2. _____

3. _____

4. _____

5. _____

Structure Note 7.8: Use 怎么 to ask how something is done.

> Subject + 怎么 + Verb Phrase

D. Using the given words as the subject, make complete sentences with the 怎么 pattern.

1. 这个蛋糕_____

2. 这个汉字_____

3. 机场_____

4. 今天中午的功课_____

5. 筷子_____

Strucutre Note 7.9: Use 往 to indicate directional movement.

> Subject + 往 + Direction + Verb

E. Fill the blanks with either 往 or 到.

1. _____ 机场，你得 _____ 西走！

2. 再 _____ 前走，你就会看到那家商店。

3. 要是 _____ 右转，我们可以先 _____ 玛丽家。

4. 我们 _____ 路口应该 _____ 左转。

5. 我要去机场，应该 _____ 哪边开？

Strucutre Note 7.10: Use 先···,再···,然后··· to indicate a sequence of events.

> Subject + 先 + Verb Phrase, + 再 + Verb Phrase, + 然后 + Verb Phrase

F. Use the words below to make sentences with the pattern: "先···,再···,然后···".

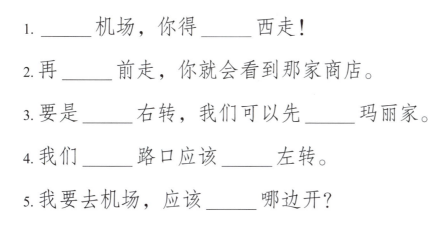

吃午饭	做功课	生日派对	买东西	回家
图书馆	看电视	看书	做饭	往左转
往右转	往前走	穿过大街	到路口	

1. _____

2. _____

3. _____

4. _____

5. _____

I. Read the following dialogue and answer the questions in Chinese.

小美：喂，大东，我是小美。
大东：小美，你好！找我有事吗？
小美：大东，我星期五要去北京，你可以送我去机场吗？
大东：你几点要到机场？
小美：中午十二点半的飞机，上午九点半到就可以了。
大东：对不起！我九点钟要上西班牙文课。
小美：没关系！那我坐出租车去吧！
大东：你什么时候回来？
小美：我下个星期六回来。
大东：那下个星期六见！
小美：再见！

1. Why does Xiaomei call Dadong?

_____

2. When does Xiaomei's flight leave?

_____

3. Can Dadong drive Xiaomei to the airport?

_____

4. How will Xiaomei go to the airport?

_____

5. When will Xiaomei come back from Beijing?

_____

II. Read the following passage and answer the questions.

玛丽的老家在波士顿，可是她爸爸是从西班牙来的，妈妈是从爱尔兰来的。她爸爸是西班牙文老师，妈妈在图书馆工作。玛丽会说英语、西班牙语，还会说汉语。寒假的时候，玛丽要回波士顿看家人，明年她要和爸爸妈妈去西班牙和爱尔兰。

1. Where is Mali's hometown?
   A. Beijing
   B. In Spain
   C. Boston
   D. California

2. Where does Mali's mother come from?
   A. Spain
   B. Ireland
   C. Boston
   D. Beijing

3. When will Mali go back to Boston?
   A. During the spring break.
   B. During the summer vacation.
   C. During the autumn break.
   D. During the winter vacation.

4. Which statement is NOT true?
   A. Mali's father is a Spanish teacher.
   B. Mali's mother is a Chinese teacher.
   C. Mali can speak three languages.
   D. Mali will travel to Spain and Ireland next year.

WRITING PRACTICE 7.2

I. Write the following sentences in Chinese or type them on your computer.

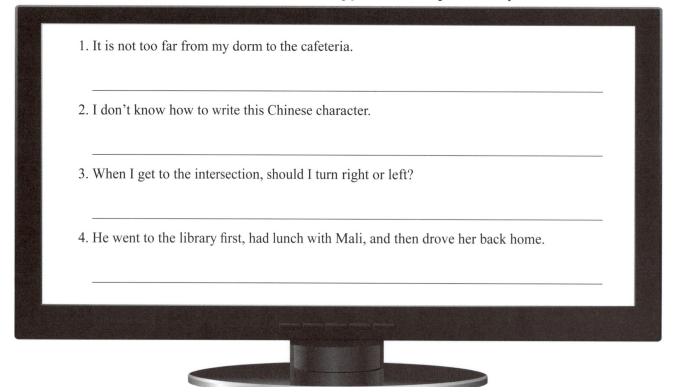

1. It is not too far from my dorm to the cafeteria.

_____

2. I don't know how to write this Chinese character.

_____

3. When I get to the intersection, should I turn right or left?

_____

4. He went to the library first, had lunch with Mali, and then drove her back home.

_____

II. E-mail Response: Zhongping plans to drive to the airport but he does not know how to get there. Read his e-mail and give him directions.

Sender	中平
Subject	机场

明天我会开车送玛丽去机场，可是我不知道机场在哪里。学校离机场远吗？从学校到机场要怎么走？

_____

_____

_____

_____

_____

_____

_____

UNIT 8 – LESSON 1

VOCABULARY REVIEW 8.1

I. Mark the correct tones above the pinyin for the vocabulary below. Read the characters aloud as you mark the tones.

1.	学期	xueqi	10.	生词	shengci
2.	选课	xuan ke	11.	比较	bijiao
3.	文学	wenxue	12.	容易	rongyi
4.	数学	shuxue	13.	觉得	juede
5.	历史	lishi	14.	进步	jin bu
6.	专业	zhuanye	15.	听懂	ting dong
7.	意思	yisi	16.	只好	zhihao
8.	年级	nianji	17.	周末	zhoumo
9.	语法	yufa	18.	练习	lianxi

II. Write the classes in Chinese characters on the lesson timetable below.

星期/时间	一	二	三	四	五
9:00 - 10:00		Chinese History	English Literature	American History	
11:00 - 12:00	Math		Chinese (Grammar)		French
13:00 - 14:00	Chinese (Listening)	Spanish		Chinese (Vocabulary revision)	

语　Radical
讠(言) yán speech
、　讠　订　讠　讦　语　语　语　语

语

法　Radical
氵(水) shuǐ water
、　氵　氵　氵　汁　泔　法　法

法

差　Radical
工 gōng work
、　丷　丷　丷　兰　羊　差　差　差

差

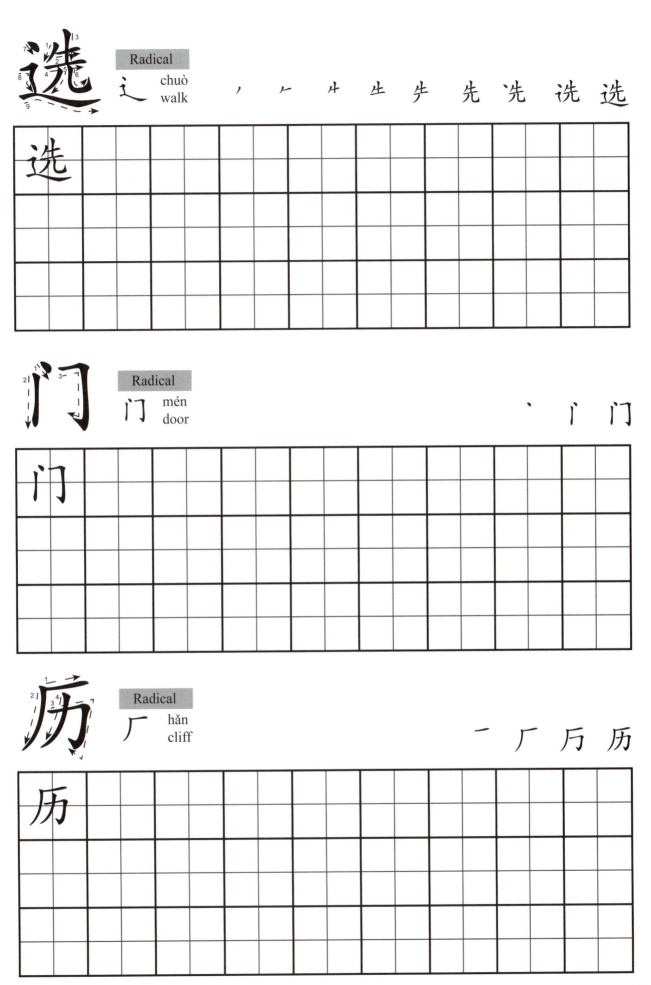

选　Radical　辶　chuò　walk　　丿　亠　屮　生　牛　先　先　选　选

门　Radical　门　mén　door　　丶　冂　门

历　Radical　厂　hǎn　cliff　　一　厂　厉　历

史

Radical
口 kǒu
mouth

、 口 口 史 史

史												

年

Radical
ノ piě
slash

ノ ㇒ ㇒ ㇒ ㇗ 年

年												

容

Radical
宀 mián
roof

、 ハ 宀 宀 宀 宀 宀 容 容

容												

易

Radical

日 rì
sun

丶 𠃌 日 日 月 易 易 易

易

听

Radical

口 kǒu
mouth

丶 𠃌 口 口 𠮛 听 听 听

听

力

Radical

力 lì
power

𠃌 力

力

觉 | Radical 见 jiàn see | 、 丶 ゛ ⺌ ⺌ 兴 兴 觉 觉

觉

步 | Radical 止 zhǐ stop | 丨 止 止 止 半 步 步

步

完 | Radical 宀 mián roof | 、 丷 宀 宀 宁 宇 完

完

I. Listen to the recording and answer the following questions.

1. How many courses did the man choose?
   A. 2   B. 3   C. 4   D. 5

2. What course did the man not choose?
   A. Math   B. Chinese   C. American History   D. English Literature

3. What is the woman's major?
   A. Math   B. Chinese   C. History   D. Literature

4. Which statement is NOT true?
   A. The man likes literature.
   B. The man sometimes cannot understand what the teacher is saying.
   C. The man thinks Chinese grammar is difficult to learn.
   D. The woman says that the man should listen to the recordings more often.

II. Listen to the recording and answer the following True or False questions.

( ) 1. The woman invites the man to her birthday party.

( ) 2. The party will be at 3 o'clock on Saturday.

( ) 3. The man will not go the party because he has to study Chinese.

( ) 4. The man thinks Chinese class is very interesting.

( ) 5. The man wants to improve his Chinese, so he needs to practice more.

III. Listen to the recording and answer the following True or False questions.

( ) 1. The woman bought many books because she is taking four courses.

( ) 2. The woman can understand French very well.

( ) 3. The woman has no time to go to a soccer game with the man.

( ) 4. The man says that the woman should listen to the recordings more often.

( ) 5. The woman will meet the man when she finishes listening to the recording.

SPEAKING PRACTICE 8.1

I. Listen to the audio recording. Say the appropriate response to each sentence that you hear. Use the space below to make note of your ideas, if necessary.

1. Your response: _____

2. Your response: _____

3. Your response: _____

4. Your response: _____

II. Make an audio recording in which you discuss your experience of studying Chinese. What level of Chinese are you taking? Is grammar easy for you or difficult? Do you like Chinese? Why? How do you try to improve your skills? Use the space below to make note of your ideas.

I. Complete the following Structure Note practices.

Structure Note 8.1: Use 懂 as a resultative complement to indicate ability to understand.

> Subject + Verb (+ 得 / 不) + 懂

A. Write the following sentences in Chinese using 懂 as a resultative complement.

1. She doesn't understand this book. _____

2. I understand the characters you wrote. _____

3. That new student doesn't understand the teacher's words. _____

4. (Create your own sentence) _____

5. (Create your own sentence) _____

Structure Note 8.2: Use 多 or 少 to express doing an activity more or less often.

> Subject + 多 / 少 + Verb Phrase

B. Make sentences in Chinese using the pattern above and the given prompts.

1. listen to the recordings _____

2. drink tea _____

3. practice Chinese _____

4. watch TV _____

5. read books _____

Structure Note 8.3: Use 只好 to indicate the the best course of action among limited options.

> Subject + 只好 + Verb Phrase

C. Complete the sentences by using 只好 according to the given hints.

1. 飞机票太贵了，我_____。(drive there)

2. 明天要考试，今天_____。(practice more)

3. 你想进步，_____。(listen to recordings more often)

4. (Create your own sentence) _____

5. (Create your own sentence) _____

Structure Note 8.4: Use Verb + 完 to describe completed actions.

Subject + Verb + 完

D. Make sentences by using 看完 / 听完 / 做完 / 写完 / 吃完 / 喝完.

1. _____

2. _____

3. _____

4. _____

5. _____

Structure Note 8.5: Use 以后 to express "after doing something."

Subject + Verb Phrase + 以后 + Verb Phrase

E. Make sentences in Chinese using 以后 and the given words.

1. （下课）_____

2. （做完功课）_____

3. （吃饭）_____

4. (Create your own sentence) _____

5. (Create your own sentence) _____

Structure Note 8.6: Use verb + 了 to describe a sequence of events.

> Subject + Verb Phrase + 了 (+ Object) + Verb Phrase

F. Make sentences in Chinese using 了 and the given words.

1. 西班牙 / 中国

   _____

2. 图书馆 / 健身房

   _____

3. 下课 / 晚饭

   _____

4. 考试 / 派对

   _____

5. 飞机 / 火车

   _____

I. Read the following passage and answer the questions.

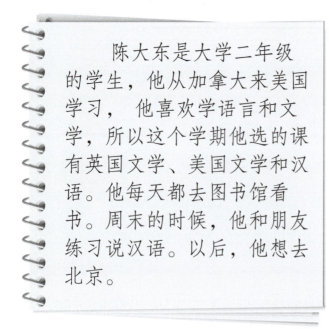

陈大东是大学二年级的学生，他从加拿大来美国学习，他喜欢学语言和文学，所以这个学期他选的课有英国文学、美国文学和汉语。他每天都去图书馆看书。周末的时候，他和朋友练习说汉语。以后，他想去北京。

1. Which statement is NOT true?
   A. Chen Dadong is a sophomore.
   B. Chen Dadong came from Beijing.
   C. Chen Dadong came to America to study.
   D. Chen Dadong likes to study languages and literature.

2. What courses is Chen Dadong NOT taking?
   A. American Literature
   B. American History
   C. British Literature
   D. Chinese

3. Which statement is true?
   A. Chen Dadong goes to the library to study everyday.
   B. Chen Dadong practices English with his friends.
   C. Chen Dadong has improved his English a lot.
   D. Chen Dadong only studies on the weekend.

II. Read the following passage and answer the True or False questions.

孙玛丽是大学一年级的学生，她想要选一门语言课。因为她喜欢中国历史，所以她想学中文。玛丽问中平："中文课很难，对不对？"中平说："一年级的中文课比较容易，语法和生词不多，可是要多听录音。"玛丽说："如果我多听录音，多练习，就会进步。明年我就可以去北京了！"所以她选中文课了。

1.   T   F   Mali is a sophomore.

2.   T   F   Mali asks Zhongping's advice about choosing Chinese class.

3.   T   F   Mali does not choose Chinese because she thinks it is too difficult.

4.   T   F   Zhongping advises Mali to listen to the recordings.

5.   T   F   Mali wants to go to Beijing.

I. Write the following sentences in Chinese or type them on your computer.

1. My major is Math. What's yours?

_____

2. How many courses did you choose this semester?

_____

3. Chinese is difficult, but it is interesting.

_____

4. If you want to improve, you have to listen to the recordings at the weekend.

_____

II. E-mail response: Mali is looking for some advice on classes. Read her e-mail and respond to her questions.

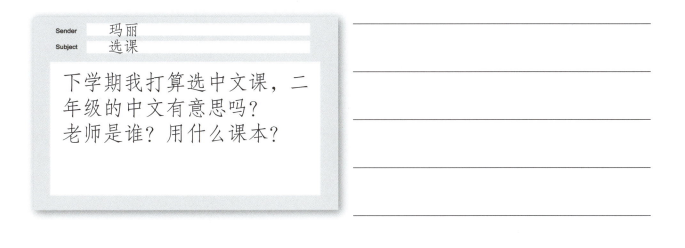

Sender 玛丽
Subject 选课

下学期我打算选中文课，二年级的中文有意思吗？
老师是谁？用什么课本？

UNIT 8 – LESSON 2

VOCABULARY REVIEW 8.2

I. Mark the correct tones above the pinyin for the vocabulary below. Read the characters aloud as you mark the tones.

1.	作业	zuoye	9.	起床	qi chuang
2.	上课	shang ke	10.	课文	kewen
3.	睡觉	shui jiao	11.	怎么办	zenme ban
4.	音乐会	yinyuehui	12.	正在	zhengzai
5.	准备	zhunbei	13.	带	dai
6.	考试	kaoshi	14.	重要	zhongyao
7.	累	lei	15.	哎呀	aiya
8.	发还	fa huan	16.	白板	baiban

II. Choose the best answers from the word box to fill in the blanks.

```
纸   准备   白板   生词   重要   笔记本
课文   正在   借   考试   觉得   忘
```

(1) _____ 上写的是下个月中文 (2) _____ 要考的

(3) _____ 和 (4) _____ 。老师说："这个考试很 (5) _____

____ ，同学们要开始 (6) _____ 了。"中平今天 (7) _____

了他的笔和 (8) _____ ，所以大东 (9) _____ 他 (10) _____

____ 和笔给他写。但是祥安 (11) _____ 这个考试不重要，所以

他 (12) _____ 睡觉。

CHARACTER WRITING PRACTICE 8.2

考

Radical

老 lǎo
old

一 十 土 耂 考 考

试

Radical

讠(言) yán
speech

丶 讠 讠 讠 讠 讠 试 试

业

Radical

一 yī
one

丨 刂 业 业 业

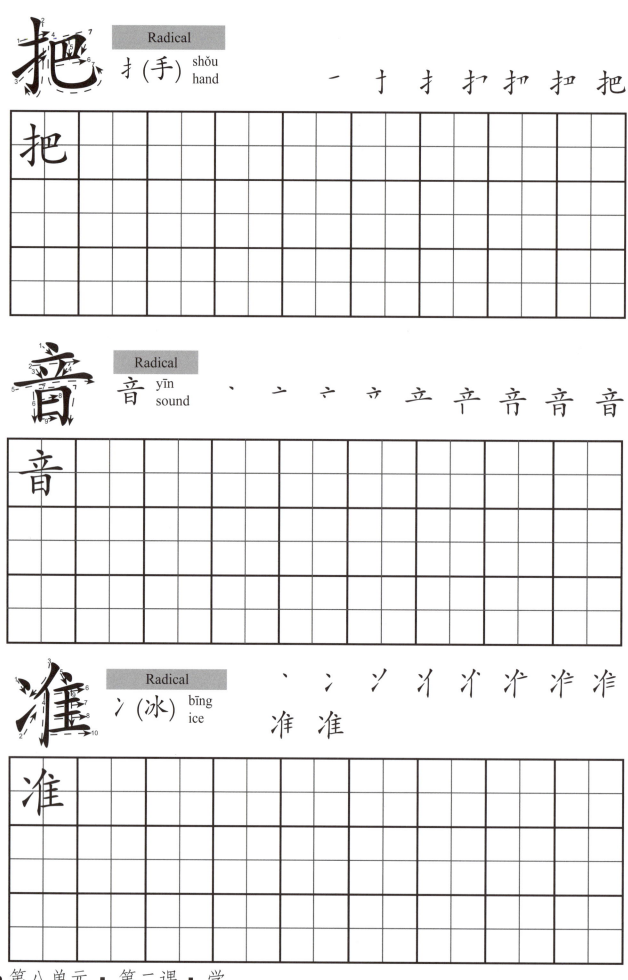

把　Radical　扌(手)　shǒu hand　　一　十　才　扣　扣　把　把

音　Radical　音　yīn sound　　丶　二　六　立　产　音　音　音

准　Radical　冫(冰)　bīng ice　　丶　冫　ソ　ィ　ォ　ゲ　ゲ　准　准　准

备

Radical

夂 zhǐ
walk slowly

ノ ク 夂 夂 各 各 备 备

備

重

Radical

里 lǐ
village

一 二 千 千 亩 亩 重 重 重

重

Radical

力 lì
power

フ 力 力 办

力

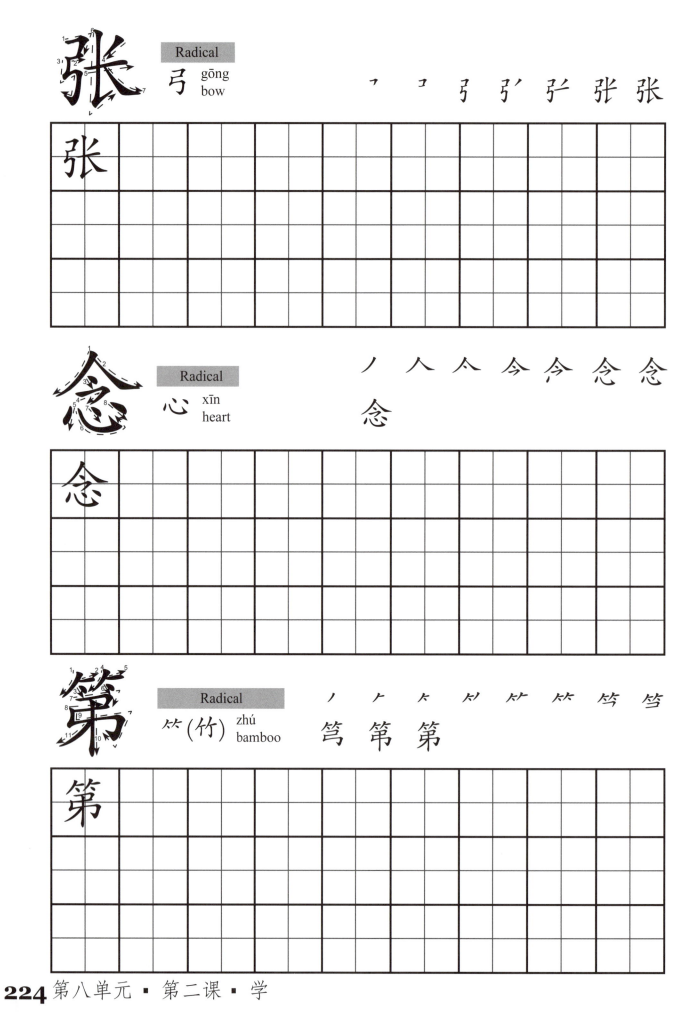

張 弓 gōng
bow
Radical

` ` ` 弓 弘 弘 弘 张 张

念 心 xīn
heart
Radical

丿 人 仒 今 令 念 念
念

第 ⺮(竹) zhú
bamboo
Radical

丿 ⺧ ⺮ ⺮ ⺮ 竺 竺 竿
笃 第 第

正 止 zhǐ stop

Radical 止 zhǐ stop

一 丁 下 正 正

白 bái white

Radical 白 bái white

ノ ィ 白 白 白

笔

Radical 竹(竹) zhú bamboo

ノ ト 大 大 竹 竹 竻 竻

竻 笔

LISTENING COMPREHENSION 8.2

I. Listen to the recording and answer the questions.

1. The conversation is between:
   A. Xiang'an and Dadong
   B. Dadong and Anna
   B. Xiang'an and his teacher
   D. Anna and her teacher

2. What does Xiang'an apologize to the teacher for?
   A. sleeping in class
   C. forgetting to bring his textbook
   B. not turning in homework
   D. borrowing a pen from a friend

3. Why is he so tired?
   A. he studied too hard the night before
   C. he went to a concert the night before
   B. he went to a soccer game the night before
   D. he got up too early

4. What time did he go to bed yesterday?
   A. 11 p.m.
   C. 2 a.m.
   B. 12 a.m.
   D. 2 p.m.

5. What did Xiang'an forget to do?
   A. go to a class
   C. prepare for a test
   B. go to a concert
   D. turn in homework

II. Listen to the conversation and answer the questions.

1. Why did the man come to class late ?
   A. He woke up too late.
   C. He doesn't like Chinese class.
   B. He forgot that he had Chinese class today.
   D. He is sick.

2. What is the teacher doing in class?
   A. reading the lesson text.
   C. teaching grammar.
   B. teaching vocabulary.
   D. teaching how to write characters.

3. What is written on the whiteboard?
   A. vocabulary for the next lesson
   C. tomorrow's lesson text
   B. grammar for this lesson
   D. test questions

4. Which statement is NOT correct?
   A. The man is late to his Chinese class.
   C. The man wants to borrow a pen.
   B. The man cannot find his textbook.
   D. The woman gives the man a piece of paper.

III. Listen to the recording and answer the following True or False questions.

(   ) 1. They will have an English test tomorrow.
(   ) 2. The man did not know what will be on the test.
(   ) 3. They will be tested on the vocabulary on lesson three.
(   ) 4. The woman will go to a concert tonight.
(   ) 5. The man will prepare the test as soon as the concert is over.

SPEAKING PRACTICE 8.2

I. Imagine that you are late for class. After arriving in class, you explain to your friend why you are late and ask him/her what you have missed. Make an audio recording of your responses and questions.

A: 你怎么这么晚才来上课？

B: _____。 _____？

A: 老师已经把第八课念完了，正在教语法。

B: _____？

A: 白板上写的是今天要做的作业。

II. Create a dialogue between you and a classmate. Imagine that you have a big test tomorrow, but you have not prepared. Make an audio recording of your responses to the prompts below. Uses the spaces provided to make note of your ideas.

A: 我们明天有考试，你准备了吗？

B: _____。 _____？

A: 我们要考语法。你要一起复习吗？我们应该在哪儿见？几点？

B: _____。

A: 你有那本语法课本吗？

B: _____。

A: 没问题，你可以借我的。考完试再找吧。

B: _____！

A: 明天见！

STRUCTURE REVIEW 8.2

I. Complete the following Structure Note practices.

Structure Note 8.7: Use 把 to indicate an action performed on a specific object.

> Subject + 把 + Object + Verb + 了 / Resultative Complement / 给 Expression

A. Fill in the blanks in the table below to make complete sentences.

	Subject	把	Object	Verb	了 / 给 / 完……
1.			作业		
2.				吃	
3.	大东	把			
4.			车票		
5.				看	

Structure Note 8.8: Use 怎么 to ask "how come" questions.

> Subject + 怎么 + Verb Phrase

B. Rewrite the following sentences in English/Chinese (using 怎么).

1. 你昨天怎么没来参加我的派对?

_____

2. 你怎么不吃青菜?

_____

3. Why did he not go home for winter break?

_____

4. Why does she dislike this book?

_____

5. How do you know where my hometown is?

_____

Structure Note 8.9: Use 怎么这么 / 那么 to express incredulity or amazement regarding a situation.

> Subject + 怎么 + 这么 / 那么 + Adjective ?

C. Complete the sentence by adding 这么 / 那么 and the appropriate adjective.

1. 你做的菜怎么_____?

2. 学校的宿舍怎么_____?

3.你昨天怎么_____才睡觉?

4.这个汉字怎么_____?

5.飞机票怎么_____?

Structure Note 8.10: Use 一···就··· to express "as soon as A, B."

> Subject + 一 + Verb Phrase (+ Subject 2) + 就 + Verb Phrase

D. Complete the following sentences using the "一···就···" pattern.

1.下课 / 回宿舍

_____

2.吃完晚饭 / 看电视

_____

3.回家 / 打电话

_____

4.上课 / 想睡觉

_____

5.放假 / 跟朋友去旅行

_____

Structure Note 8.11: Use 觉得 to express subjective opinions.

> Subject + 觉得 + Sentence

E. Write the following sentences in Chinese using 觉得.

1. Do you think Chinese is easy to learn?

_____

2. I think this restaurant is pretty good!

_____

3. I think this test is difficult.

_____

4. Do you think she will like the present I gave to her?

_____

5. She thinks the concert is more important.

_____

Structure Note 8.12: Use 还是 with adjectives to compare qualities.

> A + Adjective + 还是 + B + Adjective?

F. Rewrite the following sentences using the formula above.

1. 谁好看？玛丽还是安娜？

_____

2. 哪个好吃？烤鸭还是饺子？

_____

3. 哪个重要？考试还是派对？

_____

4. 哪儿好玩儿？北京还是波士顿？

_____

5. 哪个容易？英文还是西班牙文？

_____

Structure Note 8.13: Use 第 to express ordinal numbers.

> 第 + Number

G. Write the following phrases in Chinese using the ordinal number marker 第.

1. lesson 1 _____

2. the second year _____

3. the third Sunday of this month _____

4. the fiftieth book _____

5. the hundredth day _____

Structure Note 8.14: Use (正)在⋯⋯(呢) to indicate ongoing actions.

> Subject + (正)在 + Verb Phrase + (呢)

H. Complete the dialogues/sentences below using (正)在⋯⋯(呢).

1. A. 你在做什么？ B. _____。

2. 我回家时，妈妈_____。

3. 晚上十一点，中平还_____。

4. 老师已经说完生词了，现在_____。

5. 他来的时候，我们_____。

I. Read the following dialogue and answer the questions in Chinese.

大东：你今天怎么这么累？
祥安：我昨天晚上很晚才睡觉。
大东：你几点钟才睡觉？
祥安：十一点半。
大东：你怎么这么晚才睡呢？
祥安：我在准备第四课的生词考试。
大东：可是今天要考的是第三课。
祥安：什么！

1. Why is Xiang'an so tired?

_____

2. What time did Xiang'an go to bed last night?

_____

3. Why was Xiang'an surprised?

_____

II. Read the following passage and answer the questions.

小美星期一六点半就起床了，她八点钟要上中文课，十点有数学考试。吃完早饭，她准备笔和笔记本，就去上课了。考完试以后，玛丽想跟小美一起去吃午饭，可是小美觉得有一点儿累，她不想去吃午饭，她想先回宿舍去睡觉。

1. What time did Xiaomei have a test?
   A. 6:30 a.m.
   B. 8 a.m.
   C. 10 a.m.
   D. 12 p.m.

2. What did Xiaomei prepare for her class?
   A. pen
   B. ruler
   C. eraser
   D. all of above

3. Which statement is NOT true?
   A. Xiaomei went to her classes after breakfast.
   B. Xiaomei felt tircd after taking the test.
   C. Xiaomei had lunch with Mali.
   D. Xiaomei went back to the dorm to sleep.

WRITING PRACTICE 8.2

I. Narrate a complete story as suggested by the pictures. Give your story a beginning, middle, and an end.

_____

_____

_____

_____

_____

II. Create your own timetable. In the timetable, include classes, tests, exams, and your revision schedule.

星期/时间					